A SENSE OF MYSTERY

Compiled by
Pat Edwards &
Wendy Body

Acknowledgements

We are grateful to the following for permission to reproduce copyright material: Blackie and Son Ltd, Glasgow and London, for an extract from *The Case of the Fagin File* by Terrence Dicks; C J Fulcher on behalf of the authors, for the poems 'Ghosts in the House' by Sarah Telfer and 'Waiting' by Ruth Parker from *First Year Poetry Anthology 1986-87*, compiled by C J Fulcher, produced by Chepstow Comprehensive School; the author, Phyllis MacLennan and The Magazine of Fantasy and Science Fiction for the story 'Goodbye Miss Patterson' from *The Magazine of Fantasy and Science Fiction* © 1972 by Mercury Press, Inc; Penguin Books Ltd for the play 'The Phantom Sausage Snatcher' from *Plays for Laughs* by Johnny Ball (Puffin Books, 1983), copyright © Johnny Ball 1983, and the story 'Nule' from *Nothing to be Afraid Of* by Jan Mark (Kestrel Books, 1980), copyright © Jan Mark, 1977, 1980; Penguin Books Australia Ltd for an extract from *The Dingbat Spies* by Joan Flanagan; Scholastic, Inc for the story 'The Phantom Hound of Yorkshire' from *Amazing True Dog Stories* by Louis Sabin, copyright © 1983 by Louis Sabin and the story 'At Midnight' from *More Tales for the Midnight Hour* by J B Stamper; Stainer & Bell Ltd for the song 'Lord of the Dance', words by Sydney Carter, music adapted from an arrangement by Sydney Carter. Pages 78-9 were written by Bill Boyle and Sarah Phillips.

We are grateful to the following for permission to reproduce photographs: Australian Institute of Archaeology, page 54; Canberra Cruises Ltd, pages 82, 83; Colorsport, page 79 *below right*; Leeds City Council, pages 78/79 background, 78 *above*, 78 *below left and right*, 79 *below left*; Leeds City Tourism, page 78 *centre*; Leeds Industrial Museum, page 78 *above right*; Leeds United AFC Ltd, page 79 *above right*; Mantis Wildlife, pages 109 (photo Densey Clyne), 110 (photo Jim Frazier); Peruvian Australian Club of Victoria, page 55; Scala, page 59 The Shroud of Turin painted by Giorgio Giulio Clovio; Temple Newsam Estate, page 79 *above left*.

We are unable to trace the copyright holder of the negative photograph of the Shroud of Turin on page 58 and would appreciate receiving any information that would enable us to do so.

Illustrators, other than those acknowledged with each story, include Judith L. Mitchell pp.16-17; Geo Parkin pp.30-3; Azoo pp. 34-7 and 80-1; Rolf Heimann pp.38-9 and pp.56-7; Loui Silvestro p.46; Elizabeth Alger pp. 47-53 and 92-3; Sylvia Witte pp.60-1 and 90-1; Jenny Beck pp.62-3; Ray Micklin pp.68-9; Rachel Legge pp.102-3; Sara Woodward pp.111-12.

Contents

Nule

THE HOUSE was not old enough to be interesting, just old enough to be starting to fall apart. The few interesting things had been dealt with ages ago, when they first moved in. There was a bell-push in every room, somehow connected to a glass case in the kitchen which contained a list of names and an indicator which wavered from name to name when a button was pushed, before settling on one of them: *Parlour; Drawing Room; Master Bedroom; Second Bedroom; Back Bedroom.*

"What are they for?" said Libby one morning, after roving round the house and pushing all the buttons in turn. At that moment Martin pushed the button in the front room and the indicator slid up to *Parlour*, vibrating there while the bell rang. And rang and rang.

"To fetch up the maid," said Mum.

"We haven't got a maid."

"No, but you've got me," said Mum, and tied an old sock over the bell, so that afterwards it would only whirr instead of ringing.

The mouse-holes in the kitchen looked interesting, too.

The mice were bold and lounged about, making no effort at all to be timid and mouse-like. They sat on the draining board in the evenings and could scarcely be bothered to stir themselves when the light was switched on.

"Easy living has made them soft," said Mum. "They have a gaming-hell behind the boiler. They throw dice all day. They dance the can-can at night."

"Come off it," said Dad. "You'll be finding crates of tiny gin bottles, next,"

"They dance the can-can," Mum insisted. "Right over my head they dance it. I can hear them. If you didn't sleep so soundly, you'd hear them too."

"Oh, that. That's not mice," said Dad, with a cheery smile. "That's rats."

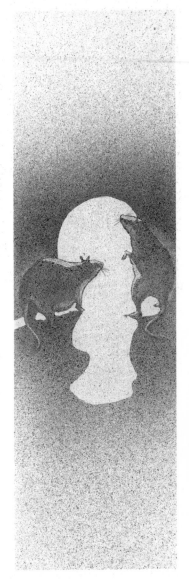

Mum minded the mice less than the bells, until the day she found footprints in the frying-pan.

"Sorry, lads, the party's over," she said to the mice, who were no doubt combing the dripping from their elegant whiskers at that very moment, and the mouse-holes were blocked up.

Dad did the blocking-up, and also some unblocking, so that after the bath no longer filled itself through the plug hole, the house stopped being interesting altogether; for a time.

Libby and Martin did what they could to improve matters. Beginning in the cupboard under the stairs, they worked their way through the house, up to the attic, looking for something; anything; tapping walls and floors, scouring cupboards, measuring and calculating, but there were no hidden cavities, no secret doors, no ambiguous bulges under the wallpaper, except where the damp got in. The cupboard below the stairs was full of old pickle jars, and what they found in the attic didn't please anyone, least of all Dad.

"That's dry rot," he said. "Thank God this isn't our house," and went cantering off to visit the estate agents, Tench and Tench, in the High Street. Dad called them Shark and Shark. As he got to the gate he turned back and yelled, "The Plague! The Plague! Put a red cross on the door!" which made Mrs Bowen, over the fence, lean right out of her landing window instead of hiding behind the curtains.

When Dad came back from the estate agents he was growling.

"Shark junior says that since the whole row is coming down inside two years, it isn't worth bothering about. I understand that the new by-pass is going to run right through the scullery."

"What did Shark senior say?" said Mum.

"I didn't see him. I've never seen him. I don't believe that there is a Shark senior," said Dad. "I think he's dead. I think Young Shark keeps him in a box under the bed."

"Don't be nasty," said Mum, looking at Libby who worried about things under the bed even in broad daylight. "I just hope we find a house of our own before this place collapses on our heads—and we shan't be buying it from the Sharks."

She went back to her sewing, not in a good mood. The mice had broken out again. Libby went into the kitchen to look for them. Martin ran upstairs, rhyming:

> *"Mr Shark,*
> *In the dark,*
> *Under the bed.*
> *Dead."*

When he came down again, Mum was putting away the sewing and Libby was parading around the hall in a

pointed hat with a veil and a long red dress that looked
rich and splendid unless you knew, as Martin did, that it
was made of old curtains.

The hall was dark in the rainy summer afternoon, and
Libby slid from shadow to shadow, rustling.

"What are you meant to be?" said Martin. "An old
witch?"

"I'm the Sleeping Beauty's mother," said Libby, and
lowering her head she charged along the hall, pointed hat
foremost, like a unicorn.

Martin changed his mind about walking downstairs and
slid down the bannisters instead. He suspected that he
would not be allowed to do this for much longer. Already
the bannister rail creaked, and who knew where the
dreaded dry rot would strike next? As he reached the
upright post at the bottom of the stairs, Mum came out of
the back room, lugging the sewing-machine, and just
missed being impaled on Libby's hat.

"Stop rushing up and down," said Mum. "You'll ruin those clothes and I've only just finished them. Go and take them off. And you," she said, turning to Martin, "stop swinging on that newel post. Do you want to tear it up by the roots?"

The newel post was supposed to be holding up the bannisters, but possibly it was the other way about. At the foot it was just a polished wooden post, but further up it had been turned on a lathe, with slender hips, a waist, a bust almost, and square shoulders. On top was a round ball, as big as a head.

There was another at the top of the stairs but it had lost its head. Dad called it Ann Boleyn; the one at the bottom was simply a newel post, but Libby thought that this too was its name; Nule Post, like Ann Boleyn or Libby Anderson.

Mrs Nule Post.

Lady Nule Post.

When she talked to it she just called it Nule.

The pointed hat and the old curtains were Libby's costume for the school play. Martin had managed to stay out of the school play, but he knew all of Libby's lines by heart as she chanted them round the house, up and down stairs, in a strained, jerky voice, one syllable per step.

"My–dear–we–must–in–vite–all–the–fair–ies–to–the–ch ris–ten–ing, Hullo, Nule, we–will–not–in–vite–the–wick–ed–fair–y! "

On the last day of term, he sat with Mum and Dad in the school hall and watched Libby go through the same routine on stage. She was word-perfect, in spite of speaking as though her shock absorbers had collapsed, but as most of the cast spoke the same way it didn't sound so very strange.

Once the holidays began Libby went back to talking

like Libby, although she still wore the pointed hat and the curtains, until they began to drop to pieces. The curtains went for dusters, but the pointed hat was around for a long time until Mum picked it up and threatened, "Take this thing away or it goes in the dustbin."

Libby shunted up and down stairs a few times with the hat on her head, and then Mum called out that Jane-next-door had come to play. If Libby had been at the top of the stairs, she might have left the hat on her bed, but she was almost at the bottom so she plonked it down on Nule's cannon-ball head, and went out to fight Jane over whose turn it was to kidnap the teddy-bear. She hoped it was Jane's turn. If Libby were the kidnapper, she would have to sit about for ages holding Teddy to ransom behind the water tank, while Jane galloped round the garden on her imaginary pony, whacking the hydrangea bushes with a broomstick.

The hat definitely did something for Nule. When Martin came in later by the front door, he thought at first that it was a person standing at the foot of the stairs. He had to look twice before he understood who it was. Mum saw it at the same time.

"I told Libby to put that object away or I'd throw it in the dustbin."

"Oh, don't," said Martin. "Leave it for Dad to see."

So she left it, but Martin began to get ideas. The hat made the rest of Nule look very undressed, so he fetched down the old housecoat that had been hanging behind the bathroom door when they moved in. It was purple, with blue paisleys swimming all over it, and very worn, as though it had been somebody's favourite housecoat. The sleeves had set in creases around arms belonging to someone they had never known.

Turning it front to back, he buttoned it like a bib

round Nule's neck so that it hung down to the floor. He filled two gloves with screwed-up newspaper, poked them into the sleeves and pinned them there. The weight made the arms dangle and opened the creases. He put a pair of football boots under the hem of the housecoat with the toes just sticking out, and stood back to see how it looked.

As he expected, in the darkness of the hall it looked just like a person, waiting, although there was something not so much lifelike as death like in the hang of those dangling arms.

Mum and Libby first saw Nule as they came out of the kitchen together.

"Who on earth did this?" said Mum as they drew alongside.

"It wasn't me," said Libby, and sounded very glad that it wasn't.

"It was you left the hat, wasn't it?"

"Yes, but not the other bits."

"What do you think?" said Martin.

"Horrible thing," said Mum, but she didn't ask him to take it down. Libby sidled round Nule and ran upstairs as close to the wall as she could get.

When Dad came home from work he stopped in the doorway and said, "Hullo—who's that? Who . . .?" before Martin put the light on and showed him.

"An idol, I suppose," said Dad. "Nule, god of dry rot," and he bowed low at the foot of the stairs. At the same time the hat slipped forward slightly, as if Nule had lowered its head in acknowledgement. Martin also bowed low before reaching up to put the hat straight.

Mum and Dad seemed to think that Nule was rather funny, so it stayed at the foot of the stairs. They never bowed to it again, but Martin did, every time he went upstairs, and so did Libby. Libby didn't talk to Nule any more, but she watched it a lot. One day she said, "Which way is it facing?"

"Forwards, of course," said Martin, but it was hard to tell unless you looked at the feet. He drew two staring eyes and a toothy smile on a piece of paper and cut them out. They were attached to the front of Nule's head with little bits of chewing-gum.

"That's better," said Libby, laughing, and next time she went upstairs she forgot to bow. Martin was not so sure. Nule looked ordinary now, just like a newel post wearing a housecoat, football boots and the Sleeping Beauty's mother's hat. He took off the eyes and the mouth and rubbed away the chewing-gum.

"*That's* better," he said, while Nule stared once more without eyes, and smiled without a mouth.

Libby said nothing.

At night the house creaked.

"Thiefly footsteps," said Libby.

"It's the furniture warping," said Mum.

Libby thought she said that the furniture was walking, and she could well believe it. The dressing-table had feet with claws; why shouldn't it walk in the dark, tugging fretfully this way and that because the clawed feet pointed

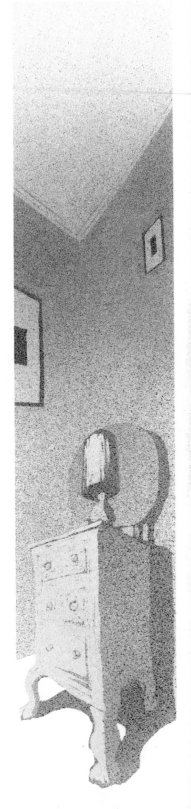

in opposite directions? The bath had feet too. Libby imagined it galloping out of the bathroom and tobogganing downstairs on its stomach, like a great white walrus plunging into the sea. If someone held the door open, it would whizz up the path and crash into the front gate. If someone held the gate open, it would shoot across the road and hit the district nurse's car, which she parked under the street light, opposite.

Libby thought of headlines in the local paper—NURSE RUN OVER BY BATH—and giggled, until she heard the creaks again. Then she hid under the bedclothes.

In his bedroom Martin heard the creaks too, but he had a different reason for worrying. In the attic where the dry rot lurked, there was a big oak wardrobe full of old dead ladies' clothes. It was directly over his head. Supposing it came through?

Next day he moved the bed.

The vacuum cleaner had lost its casters and had to be helped, by Libby pushing from behind. It skidded up the hall and knocked Nule's football boots askew.

"The Hoover doesn't like Nule either," said Libby. Although she wouldn't talk to Nule anymore she liked talking *about* it, as though that somehow made Nule safer.

"What's that?" said Mum.

"It knocked Nule's feet off."

"Well, put them back," said Mum, but Libby preferred not to. When Martin came in he set them side by side, but later they were kicked out of place again. If people began to complain that Nule was in the way, Nule would have to go. He got round this by putting the right boot where the left had been and the left boot on the bottom stair. When he left it, the veil on the hat was hanging down behind, but as he went upstairs after tea he noticed that it was now draped over Nule's right shoulder, as if Nule had turned its head to see where its feet were going.

That night the creaks were louder than ever, like a burglar on hefty tiptoe. Libby had mentioned thieves only that evening, and Mum had said, "What have we got worth stealing?"

Martin felt fairly safe because he had worked out that if the wardrobe fell tonight, it would land on his chest of drawers and not on him, but what might it not bring down with it? Then he realized that the creaks were coming not from above but from below.

He held his breath. Downstairs didn't creak.

His alarm clock gleamed greenly in the dark and told him that it had gone two o'clock. Mum and Dad were asleep ages ago. Libby would sooner burst than leave her bed in the dark. Perhaps it *was* a burglar. Feeling noble and reckless he put on the bedside lamp, slid out of bed, trod silently across the carpet. He turned on the main light and opened the door. The glow shone out of the doorway and saw him as far as the landing light switch at the top of the stairs, but he never had time to turn it on. From the top of the stairs he could look down into the hall where the street light opposite shone coldly through the frosted panes of the front door.

It shone on the hall stand where the coats hung, on the blanket chest and the brass jug that stood on it, through

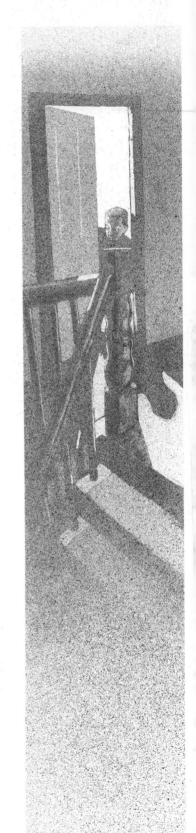

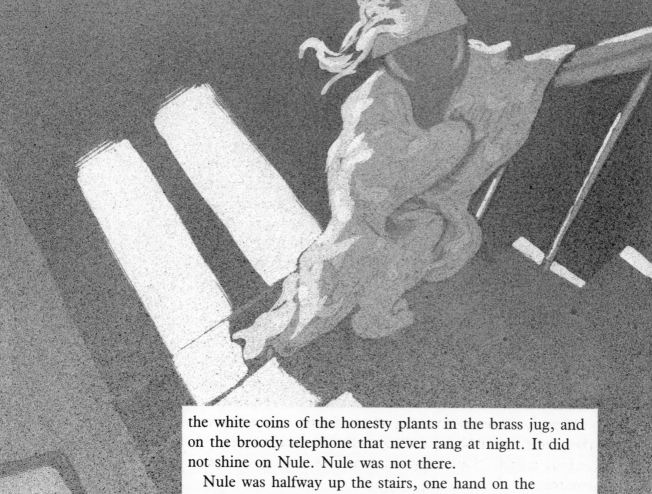

the white coins of the honesty plants in the brass jug, and
on the broody telephone that never rang at night. It did
not shine on Nule. Nule was not there.

Nule was halfway up the stairs, one hand on the
bannisters and one hand holding up the housecoat, clear of
its boots. The veil on the hat drifted like smoke across the
frosted glass of the front door. Nule creaked and came up
another step.

Martin turned and fled back to the bedroom, and dived
under the bedclothes, just like Libby who was three years
younger and believed in ghosts.

"Were you reading in bed last night?" said Mum,
prodding him awake next morning. Martin came out from
under the pillow, very slowly.

"No, Mum."

"You went to sleep with the light on. *Both* lights," she
said, leaning across to switch off the one by the bed.

"I'm sorry."

"Perhaps you'd like to pay the next electricity bill?"

Mum had brought him a cup of tea, which meant that she had been down to the kitchen and back again, unscathed. Martin wanted to ask her if there was anything strange on the stairs, but he didn't quite know how to put it. He drank the tea, dressed, and went along the landing.

He looked down into the hall where the sun shone through the frosted glass of the front door, onto the hall stand, the blanket chest, the honesty plants in the brass jug, and the telephone that began to ring as he looked at it. It shone on Nule, standing with its back to him at the foot of the stairs.

Mum came out of the kitchen to answer the phone and Martin went down and stood three steps up, watching Nule and waiting for Mum to finish talking. Nule looked just as it always did. Both feet were back on ground level, side by side.

"I wish you wouldn't hang about like that when I'm on the phone," said Mum, putting down the receiver and turning round. "Eavesdropper. Breakfast will be ready in five minutes."

She went back into the kitchen and Martin sat on the blanket chest, looking at Nule. It was time for Nule to go. He should walk up to Nule this minute, kick away the boots, rip off the housecoat, throw away the hat, but . . .

He stayed where he was, watching the motionless football boots, the dangling sleeves. The breeze from an open window stirred the hem of the housecoat and revealed the wooden post beneath, rooted firmly in the floor as it had been for seventy years.

There were no feet in the boots; no arms in the sleeves.

If he destroyed Nule, it would mean that he *believed* that he had seen Nule climbing the stairs last night, but if he left Nule alone, Nule might walk again.

He had a problem.

Written by Jan Mark
Illustrated by Mike Belshaw

Waiting

Alone. Waiting. Listening.
Footsteps can be heard from below,
Thump, thump, thump, thump.
Pitter, patter, pitter, patter, pitter, patter,
goes the rain outside
A car pulls up.
Crrrrunch, it goes on the gravel as it stops.
Bang! goes the door of the car.
Crunch, chrunch, chrunch, chrunch,
as the person walks to the door.
Knock, Knock.
Thump, thump, thump, thump.
Creeeek—as the door opens
Muffled voices can be heard.
Thump, thump, thump, thump
As they walk away
Getting quieter and quieter.
All is quiet now.
Alone, waiting, listening.

Ruth Parker aged 12

Ghosts in the House

Ghosts in the house are peeping round the door.
Ghosts in the house go tip-toeing along the floor.
Ghosts in the house are creeping slowly nearer your bed.
Ghosts in the house have scared you half to death.
Ghosts in the house are now clanking on the stair.
Ghosts in the house are giving me a scare.
Ghosts in the house whisper of the dead—
are they truly real, or are they in my head?
Ghosts in the house are really just a dream.
But this awful dream has almost made me scream.
Ghosts in the house—I'm so glad they've gone away.
I'll go to sleep now until the break of day.

Sarah Telfer aged 12

The Talking Toaster

When Mr Latimer announces that they are moving house, his wife, a dress designer, declares that she is leaving on a business trip to Budapest and the housekeeper, Mrs Donovan, promptly resigns. So the moving is left to the children: twelve-year-old Gogs (a nickname she had been given when she first started wearing glasses), and ten-year-old Toby, with a bit of hindrance from three-year-old Polly. As well as running a business consultants firm and a toy business, Mr Latimer also owns a rock group called **The Fallen Angels**. He now organises the group into driving the vans and trucks needed for the move. Roley, their leader, and Tarquin, the lead singer, become involved in helping with the unpacking and Roley finds himself taking on the job of housekeeper—his cake-only dinner is very successful!

Despite much confusion, they finally get settled, only to discover that they have moved into the wrong house: they should be in the identical one next door. Unable to face the thought of another shift, everyone is delighted when Roley suggests simply swapping numbers. They do this just before the new neighbours arrive. The children think it rather odd that all the movers appear to be sailors, but everyone is too tired to think much about it.

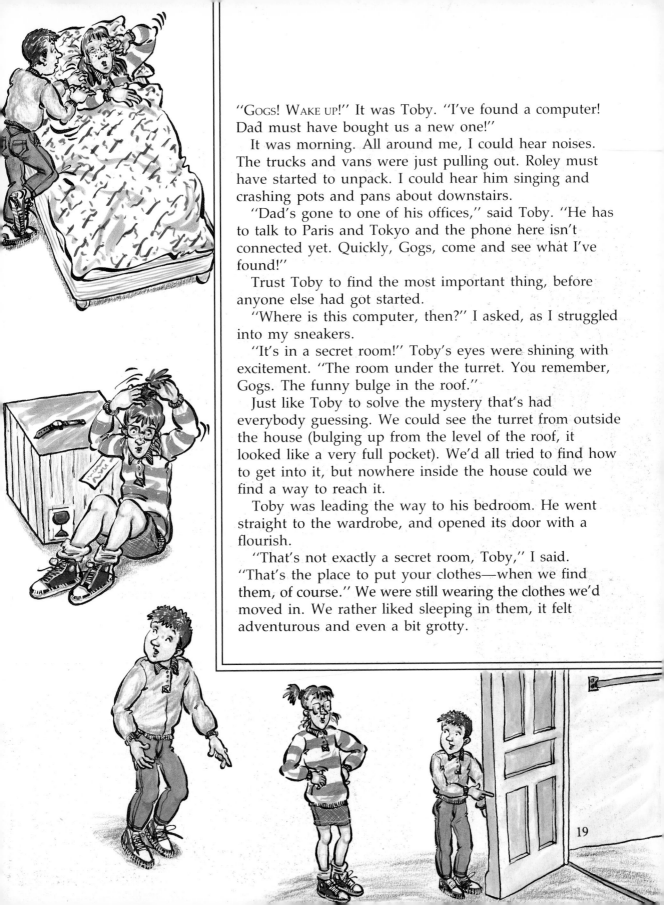

"Gogs! Wake up!" It was Toby. "I've found a computer! Dad must have bought us a new one!"

It was morning. All around me, I could hear noises. The trucks and vans were just pulling out. Roley must have started to unpack. I could hear him singing and crashing pots and pans about downstairs.

"Dad's gone to one of his offices," said Toby. "He has to talk to Paris and Tokyo and the phone here isn't connected yet. Quickly, Gogs, come and see what I've found!"

Trust Toby to find the most important thing, before anyone else had got started.

"Where is this computer, then?" I asked, as I struggled into my sneakers.

"It's in a secret room!" Toby's eyes were shining with excitement. "The room under the turret. You remember, Gogs. The funny bulge in the roof."

Just like Toby to solve the mystery that's had everybody guessing. We could see the turret from outside the house (bulging up from the level of the roof, it looked like a very full pocket). We'd all tried to find how to get into it, but nowhere inside the house could we find a way to reach it.

Toby was leading the way to his bedroom. He went straight to the wardrobe, and opened its door with a flourish.

"That's not exactly a secret room, Toby," I said. "That's the place to put your clothes—when we find them, of course." We were still wearing the clothes we'd moved in. We rather liked sleeping in them, it felt adventurous and even a bit grotty.

19

"Behold!" said Toby. He likes words like behold; he reads a lot. As he was speaking, he twiddled the rail.

The back of the wardrobe was slowly sliding sideways and as it went across I could see into the secret room that lay beyond. It was quite small, had no windows, and it looked as though it had been built to house the new computer. And what a computer! It had a keyboard, of course, and a nice big display screen and hooked up to it was a very big printer.

Stacked on shelves around the little room were the video games and the discs dad uses when he's working on the computer.

"However did you find this?"

"Well," said Toby, "I got up quite early and took a look around outside. I noticed the bulge in the roof is between two bedroom windows—yours and mine. So I came upstairs and I measured the hallway outside the bedrooms and I measured the rooms, and I figured there must be something between your wardrobe and the back of mine. So I put Polly in your wardrobe and told her to knock on the back of it and then I ran back and got into my wardrobe—and I couldn't hear any knocking."

"Oh well, I certainly could!" I said. "She very nearly woke me up."

"Then," said Toby, "I started to jiggle about inside the wardrobe and I pushed things and hit things and finally I tried twiddling the rod at the top."

"What's that banging noise!" I asked.

"Polly!" said Toby. "I forgot I'd left her in your wardrobe."

"You didn't close the outer door on her!"

"Oh yes," said Toby calmly. "I didn't want anyone to find her and ask her why she was doing that. You know how she spills the beans."

"But who'd believe her?" I asked.

"Roley might," said Toby. "Roley is getting used to believing unlikely things since dad bought him and turned him into a nanny."

I said, "A nanny? But I thought Roley was just minding us for the morning?"

"Mmm," said Toby. "I heard him joking with dad last night. He was asking would he have to wear a pinny and a frilly cap. He didn't seem to think it would look good with his leather suit and his wings."

Gosh, what a great idea. A rock singer instead of fussy old Mrs Donovan. It would make things easier for us at our new schools. The kids at the last one gave me a bad time about being picked up each afternoon by old Mrs Donovan.

Toby wasn't having much luck finding the switch that made the wall between the computer room and my wardrobe slide across.

"I know!" said Toby. "The computer must open it."

He was sitting down on the chair in front of the computer, tapping at the keyboard.

He must have asked the right sort of questions because suddenly the computer put a message up on the screen. "Hello, what can I do for you?"

This time, Toby punched in something I could understand. "Please open the door."

The computer didn't take long with that one. "It's open already."

Toby pursed his lips. "They don't usually argue with you," he said, "Whoever wrote this program did it in a very odd way."

He thought for a bit and then punched in, "Open the other door, please."

The computer came back just as quickly as it had before. "Dear goodness, can't you go out the way you came in?"

"Somebody's doing this," said Toby.

It was always possible that dad was sitting at the computer in the toy company, having a little game with us. Of course, he'd know all about the computer and the wardrobes and the secret room.

Toby was still busy. This time the message was: "My sister is locked in the wardrobe."

Suddenly the printer began to chatter furiously. I leaned over to read it, but it was spilling out lines and lines of stuff. Paper came spooling down onto the floor as the printer chattered out its endless message.

"Oh dear," said Toby. "That must be a code phrase the computer has been programmed to recognize. Just look at all that stuff."

We picked up the printout, but couldn't make much sense out of it. It was something about cleaning up the world after sombody dropped something messy on it.

Just then, the printer stopped its whacky chattering.

"Oh rats!" said Toby, but he didn't stay exasperated for long because suddenly the door on the far wall began to slide back and there was Polly, one of my thongs raised to knock, gazing at a wall which was fast disappearing. She didn't seem too surprised. I suppose living with our family knocks the surprise out of you.

The computer was active again. The printer began to chatter again, but this time it was only a short burst.

Toby and I peered at the paper to see what it had written. It was "Disregard last message".

"We'd have to," I said. "Since we couldn't understand a word of it."

Polly was gazing at the computer. "What games does it play?" she asked. "Does it do Star Wars of the Milky Way?" That's her favourite.

"Sure to," I said.

"Never mind that now," said Toby. "We'd better get out of here before anyone finds out what we've been doing."

"But, Toby," I said, "we must tell everyone what we've found."

"Trust me for a bit, Gogs," said Toby. "There's something I . . . Well, it's the house. I think we'd better see what other secrets it's got to hide."

He sent me and Polly to the kitchen and said he'd take a careful look around the living room. "Call me if you find anything," he said.

I called after him as he bustled off. "But what are we looking for?"

Toby came back to the kitchen door. "Oh, I don't know. Anything that isn't as it ought to be."

Well, that was a pretty tall order in a house with furniture and packing cases dumped every which way. The kitchen seemed a reasonable place to start searching though. It was now clear of packing cases because Roley had obviously made a start there. And most of the furniture, of course, was built in.

I followed Polly to the bench near the stove, and was just in time to stop her trying to cut herself a slice of one of last night's cakes. She really likes cake.

"Where's the cake man?" she asked as I took the knife from her.

"Roley's probably going to give us some breakfast soon," I said.

But she'd lost interest in Roley. And in the cake. She was chattering to the toaster. "Are you still there, Troll?" she was saying.

I said, "Why are you talking to the toaster?"

She blinked at me. "It talked to *me*," she said.

"When?" I asked.

"When I was in here before," she said. "There's a troll inside it."

23

Control calling Waterlily...

I was just about to give her a little talk about making up stories when the toaster began to chatter.

"Control calling Waterlily. Come in Waterlily. Do you read me, Waterlily? Come in please. Come in."

"Coming!" Polly was beginning to climb up on the stool near the bench.

I pulled her back down to the kitchen floor. And that takes some doing. Polly is a chunky little girl.

"What did you think you were doing?" I asked.

"I was going to get inside the toaster," she said."

"You can't," I said. "You won't fit."

"The troll did," she said.

Of course! Polly knows what a troll is because the Latimer Toy Company sells whole families of troll dolls— squat ugly dolls, with frowns on their faces.

I said, "He's not saying Troll, Polly; he's saying Control", but I didn't get any further because suddenly the back door opened and Roley came in. Sure enough, he'd been to the supermarket. He began to unpack plastic bags full of eggs, bread, milk, honey. Stuff for breakfast.

"Now then, chicks," he said. "What's the buzz?"

"The toaster is talking to us, Roley," I said.

He was just about to tell me it wasn't, when suddenly, once again, it was.

"Control calling Waterlily. Control calling Waterlily." The toaster never gave up.

"Ah yes," said Roley. I could see he was thinking hard.

"Well," he said, after quite a long pause, "What we have here, I would say, is the toaster picking up a freak broadcast. Tarquin has been known to pick up Radio 10WS on his tooth."

I said, "How come our toaster has never freaked like this before?"

Toby's voice suddenly came from the kitchen door. "Because that's not our toaster. This one is much bigger than ours. I think it must have been in the house when we got here."

"He's right!" said Roley. "I believe I saw it sitting on the bench the first time I came into the kitchen."

24

"Toast!" said Polly happily. "Roley can be the toast mister!"

Polly has a trick of hearing only the words that really matter to her.

"What's that?" asked Roley.

"She's got it mixed up with toastmaster," I said. "Dad was the toastmaster at a dinner last week, so when Polly heard him talking about it, she got the idea he'd spent the whole evening making toast."

"Yes," she said. "Toast." But she was beginning to sound a little dispirited. I think she thought there'd been too much talk and not enough cooking.

"She's hungry," said Roley. "And breakfast is coming up very soon. But, first of all, we'd better silence the infernal talking toaster."

Toby reached out quickly and disconnected the toaster's plug.

"Hello, where's the little chick going?" asked Roley.

Polly was heading for the door to the hallway. "I'm going to talk to the Pie Mister," she said.

Roley looked at me for an explanation, but "Pie Mister" was a new word for Polly.

"I think she must mean one of her made-up people," I said, but then I noticed she was looking very stormy, putting on what mum calls her 'square mouth'. Polly is pretty, but when she puts on the square mouth she *can* look a little bit ugly.

She doesn't like you to say that you don't believe in her imaginary people.

"He isn't made up," she said. "The Pie Mister is real. He talks to me on the telephone in my room."

"Oh that's her toy telephone," said Toby. "The pink one, is it, Polly? The one with the flowers and birds all over it."

Polly looked a little blank. "The pink one," she said and bustled off.

"She's always talking on that toy telephone," I said. "She talks to rabbits and pixies and elves and stuff like that."

"Let her go," said Toby. "Talking on the telephone is good for her. It calms her down."

25

When we were out of Roley's earshot, Toby asked "Did you find anything odd?"

"Well, the toaster seemed a bit odd," I said. "Wouldn't you say?"

"I found a telephone," said Toby.

"Well, that's not so odd," I said. "That will be ours. It's due to be connected soon."

"No," said Toby. "This one was in the cupboard by the side of the fireplace. The cupboard for the firewood. Gogs, can't you hear it? It's ringing now!"

I couldn't hear anything at first, but when I put my head down next to the door of the little wood cupboard, I could hear the faintest sound. Brrp . . . Brrp . . .

I put my hand to the cupboard door.

"No, Gogs," Toby sounded quite excited. "Don't answer it!"

I stopped. "Whyever not?"

"Because," said Toby. "Because there's something odd about it. Don't you realize? There's a telephone in the hallway. And that should be ringing too. But it *isn't*."

He is quick-witted. Of course I'd seen the telephone in the hallway. I hadn't even noticed that it wasn't ringing.

"How did you ever manage to hear it?" I asked. "The bell is so soft!"

"Well," said Toby, "you see, it rang before. And I didn't hear it that time, exactly. I *saw* it!" He pointed to his watch.

The light on his digital watch—the light you switch on when you want to see the time in the dark—well, it was pulsing on and off, keeping time with the telephone bell.

"I noticed it the first time when the light flashed into my eyes," Toby explained.

I said, "Answer it, Toby. We can pretend it's a wrong number and hang up."

"We won't need to pretend," said Toby. "It *is*. I answered it the first time and an American voice barked at me. Didn't even give me time to say our name and our telephone number. And what it said, the voice . . . well, it was rubbish. It said, 'The caterpillar is chasing the guinea pig and it's due to catch it when the porcupine has a coughing fit!'"

"Let's go and tell Roley."

"Hang on a minute, Gogs," said Toby.

But I was in a hurry to tell Roley what had happened.

Toby followed me to the kitchen, but when we got there we forgot about the telephone because Roley was standing at the big kitchen window (it looked into the yard of the house next door) watching an amazing scene.

The yard next door was full of sailors in uniform rushing about with furniture and stuff. They must have delivered another load while Toby and I were busy with our investigations.

"What do you make of that, you guys?" asked Roley.

And that's when Toby dropped his bombshell. (You can see which of our parents he takes after.)

"Another lot of sailors are helping the spies move in," said Toby.

"The what?" shouted Roley.

"I think I should tell you both," said Toby, solemnly. "The people next door—the people whose house we've stolen—well, they're all spies!"

"Spies?" said Roley. "You're putting me on!"

"No, I'm not," said Toby. "It's true. Some kids told me. Paperboys, they were."

"But you haven't had time to talk to any kids in this neighbourhood," I said.

"Why not?" asked Toby. "By now, dad's had time to talk to London and Paris."

"These mysterious paperboys you met this morning told you the house next door is a nest of spies?" Roley looked disbelieving.

"No," said Toby. "They told me this house was."

Oops. That put a new light on the house swap.

27

"They're not very good spies," Toby said. "They've been sent here, in secret, to be retrained. They're spies who are really bad at their jobs."

"Yes, they must be," said Roley. "They haven't noticed yet they're in the wrong house."

"Well, you see," said Toby. "What they were expecting to move into was something called a 'safe house'."

"I've read about those," I said. "In spy stories. Spies use safe houses for resting up after dangerous missions, and for spying lessons."

"How did the guys with the paper route find out about the spies?" asked Roley.

"Oh, everyone around here knows," said Toby. "The lady in the post office says she found out weeks ago, and she told them."

"Does she know we've moved into the spies' house?" I asked.

"And do the spies know?" asked Roley.

"They're sure to find out," said Toby, "When they go looking for their computer. Well, at least they'll find out they're in the wrong house, and since there are only two houses in the crescent, and as this one is exactly . . ."

Roley held up his hand to stem the flow of logic.

"Did I hear the word computer?" he asked.

Toby explained what he'd found behind the wardrobes.

"Ah, well," said Roley. "Perhaps things aren't so serious after all. It just so happens your father had your computer delivered yesterday afternoon and installed in a turret room. We can only suppose the people who brought it took it into the house next door. So, you see, when the spies go to tickle the keyboard of their computer, they'll find your computer and it could be they won't realize . . ."

"No good, Roley," I said. "Toby, tell him about the secret telephone in the wood cupboard."

Oh yes," said Roley. "And I suppose I'd better tell *you* about the cordless yellow telephone I found in the breadcrock."

I glanced quickly across at Toby.

But it was obvious that he hadn't yet found the phone in the breadcrock.

"Let's take a look at the computer and the secret room," said Roley, leading the way to the staircase.

As we passed Polly's room, we heard a phone ringing and we all froze. It was in her room. And it was a real phone. It wasn't the noise her elves' telephone makes when people pretend to ring it. That sounds like a stick being dragged across an iron railing. This was a telephone bell, louder than the one in the wood cupboard.

"Don't answer it!" Toby shouted.

"That was the Pie Mister," she said, with a pout.

"She's really getting her words mixed up this morning," I said.

"No, no," said Polly crossly. "That's his name. He told me."

Suddenly Roley's expression changed from its usual smiling peaceful look to one of intense shock.

"Polly!" His voice sounded quite sharp. I'd never heard it that way before. "Tell me exactly what the man said to you—the man on the phone."

Polly thought for a bit, and then she said,"He said go at once and get your daddy."

That's not the sort of thing Polly's imaginary people usually say to her," I said.

"No, you're right," said Toby thoughtfully. "No, they usually rabbit on about dollies and playdough and stuff."

Roley said, "Now then, Polly what did this man say when he told you who he was?"

Polly had the answer ready to that one. She said, "He said to me, "Little boy, do you realize you are talking to the Pie Mister?""

And suddenly it hit all of us.

"Suffering catfish," said Roley. "This little chick has been talking to the Prime Minister!"

Written by Joan Flanagan
Illustrated by Maggie Ling

Who dunnit?

That's the million dollar question!

Private Eye, Sally Smart suddenly startled her companions by whipping a wig from the man's head, revealing a crop of bright red hair. "It was you, Higgins, wasn't it?" she said. "It was you who killed the prime minister!"

Higgins looked as if he might make a run for it, but a quick glance at the alert policeman standing at the door told him he had no chance. He collapsed in a chair.

"Yes, it was me," he said brokenly. "But how . . . how did you know?"

"One red hair in the victim's hand," said Sally. "I'd noticed one just like it on your coat collar when I came to view the body. That was the first clue. Then the angle of the shot told me that the murderer had to be left-handed and I saw that you used your left hand when you stirred your tea while we were discussing the crime. But the main clue was . . ."

That's the way all crime programmes and detective stories seem to end, isn't it? The detective or super sleuth explains how he or she put all the clues together and worked out the solution to the crime.

Millions of murder mystery books are sold all around the world every year. And it's a rare night on television that some detective is not relentlessly tracking down a murderer. Why are they so popular? Perhaps it's the thrill of feeling close to danger, when you know that you are quite safe. Or perhaps it's the satisfaction of trying to work out the puzzle before the book or television programme tells you.

The rules never change. There's always at least one victim who gets murdered and a detective who patiently works through the clues, looking for evidence, trying to find out if the murdered person said anything before he or she died, testing the murder weapon for fingerprints, hunting for witnesses who may not want to be found . . . And nine times out of ten, the criminal is the person you least suspected.

Why do people call detective stories "Who dunnits"?

It is a catchy way of describing a book in which the plot is built around the question "who did the murder?".

When did authors first start writing detective novels?

The first ever detective story was *The Murders in the Rue Morgue* by American writer Edgar Allan Poe. It was published in a magazine around 1842. The first detective novel is thought to be Wilkie Collins' *The Moonstone* which came out in 1868. Certainly it is known to be the first English detective story.

For a time, lots of cheap mysteries were churned out. They were called "penny-dreadfuls" — they looked cheap and nasty and only cost one penny. But gradually, more and more writers got interested in this type of story and the quality began to get better. It was probably Sir Arthur Conan Doyle who really made the detective story respectable — and incredibly popular. Once he'd invented Sherlock Holmes everyone wanted to try writing a detective story. Gradually, the world of fiction became peopled with a weird and wonderful collection of sleuths. Some were attached to the police force, some were scientists, some were private detectives (or "private eyes" as they became known), some were wealthy people who unravelled mysteries as a hobby. After Sherlock Holmes, the next most famous detective is probably the Belgian, Hercule Poirot. He solves his crimes by using "the little grey cells of his brain" — in other words by carefully putting all the clues in their right order. His inventor, Agatha Christie, also created an elderly lady detective, Miss Marple, who solves her crimes by studying the suspects' behaviour.

There are certain novels that are considered to be the classics of the detective story world. Some examples are:

The Murders in the Rue Morgue by Edgar Allan Poe,
The Moonstone by Wilkie Collins,
The Mystery of the Handsome Cab by Fergus Hume,
The Redhaired Gang by Arthur Conan Doyle,
Murder on the Orient Express by Agatha Christie,
The Nine Tailors by Dorothy Sayers.

There are also classic mysteries such as *The Gold Bug* by Edgar Allan Poe, *The 39 Steps* by John Buchan and *Coffin for Demetrios* by Eric Ambler. Have you read any of them?

WANT TO WRITE

Why not try your hand at writing a murder mystery? Who knows, you might be the writer the world is waiting for . . . a new Agatha Christie perhaps?

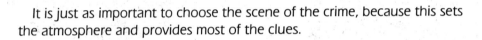

First you have to decide on:
(a) the victim,
(b) the murderer and
(c) the detective.

It is just as important to choose the scene of the crime, because this sets the atmosphere and provides most of the clues.

How's this for an example? Your school headmaster opens the staffroom door one sunny morning and finds a dead body lying on the floor. The scene of the crime is set!

Now, who is the victim? The deputy or one of the teachers? The caretaker or a cleaner? One of the pupils? One of the parents? A perfect stranger? Take your pick.

A MYSTERY?

Where to go from there?

Weave your mystery into a tight web by deciding on your murderer and then working through these points:

The method: Was the victim shot (with a gun or bow and arrow)? Strangled or hanged? Poisoned? Stabbed (pocket knife, paper knife, dagger, ice pick)? Battered with a blunt instrument (club, brick or stone, chair leg)? Smothered, perhaps?

The motive: Why was this person murdered?

Was it premeditated? That is, did the murderer plan the crime carefully because she or he had something to gain? Money to inherit? Was the victim dangerous in some way — a blackmailer or accomplice or even an innocent witness to another crime the murderer had committed?

Was it unpremeditated, something that happened accidentally? Did the victim discover the murderer in the midst of a robbery and get struck down when the murderer panicked? Was the victim mistaken for someone else? Did the murderer go to the wrong address and kill before realising the mistake?

The detective or sleuth: Is she or he someone working with the police force? A private eye (perhaps the head's niece or nephew who's visiting at the moment)? One of the staff? A clever pupil?

Now you can play around with the plot, depending on what motive you've chosen. Work out what the clues are to be — fingerprints on a paper knife or cup? A scrap of paper clutched in the victim's hand, bearing a mysterious phone number or address that can be traced to the murderer? A witness who glimpsed the number plate of a car seen speeding from the scene of the crime? Initials scrawled in the dust by the dying victim? There are lots of possibilities!

Of course, your detective must discover and untangle these one by one. If you are clever, you'll make sure most of the clues could apply to more than one person. For example, the initials MT could apply to a teacher named Mary Thomas, to pupil Mike Taylor, or even to head Mervin Tremblow. And that car could have been borrowed or stolen!

But remember you must play fair. It must all work out neatly in the end with the detective triumphantly solving the puzzle and the murderer being marched off to jail.

Thought of a title? How about *The Staffroom Murder?* Or *The Case of the Stolen Stapler* or *Who Killed the Head's Favourite Pupil?*

Pat Edwards

SCOTLAND YARD

In television crime programmes or detective novels, sooner or later a detective from "The Yard" will be called in. Where did the name come from?

In 1829, the British government decided to build offices for the first Commissioner of Police for metropolitan London. The site chosen was that of an old palace which had been used by visiting Scottish royalty in the days before England and Scotland were one kingdom. Because of this, the new building became known as Scotland Yard and the name stuck so that when they later moved to larger offices the name went along too and the new headquarters were officially called New Scotland Yard.

It was 1842 before Scotland Yard set up its own Criminal Investigation Department. Up till then, the detective work was done by fifteen men called the Bow Street Runners. They were more like private detectives and had to be paid before they agreed to take on a case.

Scotland Yard is actually the police force for London only. Other police forces in the provinces often ask "The Yard" detectives for help in solving a difficult case and usually the help is never refused. But they must be invited. Scotland Yard has no right or power to interfere in a case outside the London area.

What do you make of it, SIR ARTHUR?

Who was Sir Arthur?

It's elementary my dear readers!

Arthur Conan Doyle was born in Edinburgh, Scotland in 1859. His first area of interest was medicine and it was during his studies that he met an amazing real-life character called Dr Joseph Bell. Arthur was most impressed with the doctor's clever way of thinking and reasoning. (I wonder what Dr Bell thought when Arthur later turned him into the famous Sherlock Holmes!)

Why did Sir Arthur turn to writing?

Well it seems that young Arthur grew tired of medicine and playing doctor, so he tried his hand at writing. In 1887, he introduced Sherlock Holmes and his trusty side-kick Dr Watson, to an avid band of readers. Their popularity grew.

Through book after book, Holmes the super-clever detective, prowled the dark foggy streets of London, solving mystery after mystery and crime after crime. And from time to time, he was helped by a group of young people known as the Baker Street Irregulars.

Hmmmmmmmmm

But all good things must come to an end. Arthur grew tired of constantly writing about Sherlock Holmes. In the last tale, he had Sherlock fall off a cliff . . . but Sherlock's popularity refused to die. In 1904, (after he was knighted), Sir Arthur once more picked up his pen and brought the famous detective back to life in three more books.

Sir Arthur Conan Doyle didn't put his pen away entirely. He went on to write historical novels, and before his death in 1930, he promised he'd tell the most amazing tale of all, *after* his death. He planned to return from the land of the dead with the greatest mystery of them all unravelled — he planned to tell what "life" was like on the other side! Well, Sir Arthur, what did you make of it?

We're still waiting to hear . . .

Margarette Thomas-Cochran

The Burglar

Dan and his three teenage friends, Jeff, Liz and Mickey, model themselves on the Baker Street Irregulars, the young helpers of Sherlock Holmes. Their friend, Detective Constable Day, has asked them to keep their eyes and ears open in the hope of picking up some clues about a series of burglaries in their London district. They decide to start a rumour that a lot a money will be locked up overnight in the rickety old safe in their headmaster's office. Then the four friends visit the school that evening to see if the burglar will take the bait ...

It was dark in the school.

Crouched in the corner of the corridor outside the headmaster's study, hiding behind a stack of paper-filled tea-chests, Dan thought how sinister the place seemed after hours. The familiar classrooms and corridors were shadowed and gloomy. It was easy to imagine the giant figure of Frankenstein's monster stretched on a bench in the science labs, stirring beneath its covering sheet, sitting jerkily upright ... You could imagine it lumbering out of the laboratory and lurching towards you ...

Dan jumped as a bony elbow jabbed him in the ribs and Mickey's voice hissed, "Someone's coming!" Heavy footsteps were coming down the corridor towards them, thump, thump, thump ... The thing was casting a huge shadow before it. Dan half-expected to see a giant square-headed figure with a bolt through its neck come staggering around the corner ...

The figure that did appear was very different, short, tubby and bald-headed with a straggling moustache. It was old Pop Daniels the school caretaker, who was both short-sighted and bad-tempered. Dan and Mickey crouched down behind the boxes as Pop stumped along the corridor and disappeared around the corner.

"What do you bet that's it for the night?" whispered Dan.

Mickey nodded. "Serve them right if all the money does get pinched," he said indignantly. Mickey had told the story so many times he believed it himself.

They had been waiting for a couple of hours and apart from the scare with old Pop nothing much had happened. Liz and Jeff were out in the playground keeping watch on the window of the study. Dan reckoned it was less likely that the thief would come that way — if he came at all, that was — since the window was visible from the street, but they had to cover it. As Mickey said, "We'd look a right lot of nits, hiding outside the door while the thief came through the window!"

They'd taken up their vigil straight after school, using the simple method of staying behind and hiding. Mickey had wanted to come back in the middle of the night, but Dan pointed out that a lot of the robberies had taken place in the early evening, and they'd never get away with staying out all night anyway. As it was, each of their parents thought they were spending the evening at Dan's house.

Meanwhile Liz and Jeff were hiding behind the climbing tree in the school playground. Jeff was pretty disgruntled since he too reckoned it was unlikely the thief would try this way. The school was a rambling old building with plenty of doors and windows. It was pretty certain that any thief would get in somewhere else and approach the study from the inside.

Or so they thought. Suddenly Liz grabbed Jeff's arm. "Look!" For a second the street that ran alongside the school was empty — and at just that moment a figure slipped over the school gates and disappeared into a shadowy corner of the playground. The shape was so thin and dark, and it moved so quickly it looked almost like a shadow itself, and for a moment they lost sight of it. Then it appeared again scuttling along the wall towards the window of the headmaster's study.

Jeff and Liz watched in fascination. There was an almost animal-like quality about the intruder's movements, the quick scurry and freeze that you usually see only in mice and squirrels.

The dark shape climbed up to the broad stone windowsill and froze again. After a moment they saw its hands moving busily, presumably forcing the catch, then it opened the window a little at the bottom and slipped through the gap.

Jeff and Liz looked at each other in astonishment.

They'd never really expected to see a burglar and they had no real idea of what to do now that they had. They began creeping closer to the window . . .

Dan fished for a sandwich from his haversack. Perhaps the plan wasn't going to work after all. He saw Mickey holding out a hand in silent appeal. He'd scoffed all his provisions in the first few minutes. Dan grinned and passed him a cheese sandwich.

Dan yawned, and his head began to nod. He shook it to wake himself up, stared hard at the study door — and saw a brief flash of light from beneath it. He nudged Mickey. "There's someone in there!"

Mickey nearly choked on his cheese sandwich. "There can't be. We didn't hear anything."

"Maybe we didn't. But there's someone in the study, using a torch."

"What do we do?"

"We find out who it is."

Dan moved quietly to the study door and flung it open. He saw a dark figure crouching by the headmaster's desk shining a torch around the room. It whirled and sprang for the open window — and cannoned into Jeff, who was climbing in from the outside. The figure turned, dodged around Dan, ran for the study door — and tripped over Mickey, who was running in after Dan.

Dan hurled himself on to the prone figure and Jeff jumped on top of him. By the time Liz came through the window there was a struggling heap of bodies in the middle of the floor. Deciding there was no point in adding another to the pile, Liz walked calmly over to the door and switched on the light.

The heap of bodies thrashed around a little longer, and then resolved itself into Dan and Jeff holding down a third boy. Mickey, who'd been on the bottom of the pile, had wriggled free and stood gasping for breath.

Now the light was on they could all get a good look at their captive. He didn't look very fearsome. He was thin and dark with close-cropped hair, and he wore black jeans, black plimsolls, a black sweater, and a black imitation-leather windcheater. It was difficult to tell his age. The thin scrawny body wasn't much bigger than Mickey, but the narrow suspicious face with the watchful eyes seemed to belong to someone older than any of them.

Dan and Jeff got up, heaving their prisoner on to his feet.

"Well now," said Dan. "What's all this about?"

The answer was a string of four-letter words. Jeff, who had old fashioned views about swearing in front of ladies, gave their prisoner a shake. "Oy, pack that up, or you'll get a thick ear. What are you doing here?"

The prisoner said nothing.

"You wouldn't have heard a rumour about there being a lot of money in the school?" asked Dan.

Still the prisoner didn't speak.

"Search him, Mickey," ordered Dan.

The lad begun struggling wildly, but Dan and Jeff held him fast. Mickey went quickly through his pockets, and produced a torch, a comb, some loose change, a couple of crumpled pound notes, a folded scrap of paper, a handkerchief and a tightly-rolled cloth bundle. He laid out his finds on the headmaster's desk.

Dan unfolded the piece of paper. It contained a sketch-map of the school and grounds with the headmaster's study clearly marked. He unrolled the bundle. It was a long strip of cloth divided into pockets, rather like the larger version of the traditional 'housewife' for carrying needles and thread. But this housewife held a variety of tools, including a drill, several small crowbars, hacksaws and files, and a set of skeleton keys. "The complete burglar's do-it-yourself kit," murmured Dan. "You certainly came well prepared."

"Shall I dial 999?" asked Mickey excitedly.

"Not yet." Dan looked hard at their sullen prisoner. "Look, if we do call the police, you're in big trouble. Burglar's tools, a map. But we're not all that interested in you. We want to know who's behind this, and all the other robberies."

"We want Mr Big," said Mickey in his tough voice.

"Tell us who it is, and we'll let you go," said Dan persuasively. "They needn't even know we got you. You can go back and say there was nothing here. There isn't you know — we made that story up just to catch you."

"No cash?"

"There might be a few quid milk money, somewhere, but that'd be all."

"But Fagin said — "the prisoner stopped himself.

Still in the same quiet voice Dan said, "Fagin?"

"Fagin's just a nickname, innit? Sort of joke."

"Tell us his real name then. Just the name and we'll let you go."

"May I inquire what is going on here, Robinson?" An all-too-familiar figure was standing in the doorway. It was the headmaster — popularly known in the school as Old Fusspot.

Everyone turned in astonishment, and the prisoner seized his chance. With a savage jerk he freed himself from their grip, streaked across the room and disappeared through the open window.

Written by Terrence Dicks
Illustrated by Debby Strauss

THE SECRET
of the
PHARAOH'S PYRAMID

In ancient times, Egypt was ruled by the pharaohs. One of the wealthiest and most powerful of these was Rameses III. His store of gold and silver was so great that it was talked about far and wide. In time, Rameses III became more and more alarmed that someday someone would come and steal his treasure from him.

He decided to summon his master builder. "Build me a great treasure house," he commanded, "with walls so thick no man may ever pierce them".

All the stone-masons of ancient Egypt set to work. Under the care and direction of the master builder, the great treasure house took shape. Its floor was of solid rock, its walls were metres thick and they were shaped into the tall peaked roof of a great pyramid.

Deep in the centre of this impregnable building was the treasure chamber. And when it was filled to capacity with all the gold, silver and precious objects you could imagine, the great iron doors at the entrance to the pyramid were sealed. They were to be opened strictly on the pharaoh's orders only.

But the master-builder had cleverly double-crossed his pharaoh. He had secretly built a second passage to the treasure chamber and he sealed it, at either end, with two stone doors which silently swivelled on pivots when their secret springs were released. When closed, these doors were indistinguishable from the surrounding walls.

Now the master-builder was not a greedy man so the pharaoh didn't notice the slight and gradual decline in his riches. But some time after the completion of the pyramid, the master-builder fell ill and died. Only on his death-bed did he whisper his secret to his two sons.

As soon as the master-builder had been buried and the proper period of mourning was over, the two sons lost no time in recovering from their grief. It proved so easy for them to enter and leave the treasure chamber, and so fantastic were the riches it contained, that they simply could not resist returning again and again and again.

The pharaoh was astonished when he realised that his great wealth was slowly and surely declining, week by week. Though he could not understand why the seals on the great iron doors were never broken, he decided to catch the thief. With some of his most trusted advisors he arranged for a deadly trap to be set among the piles of gold and silver.

On their very next visit, the first brother to gather up a sackful of gold was caught and held fast.

"Dearest brother!" he cried, "It is the end for me. And for you and all our family unless you do as I say. The pharaoh is sure to torture me cruelly. I beseech you! Kill me swiftly with your sword. Cut off my head and take it away with you so that our family may never be suspected."

When the chamber was opened next day, the headless body of the thief was found to the great amazement of the pharaoh! But thinking over the strange event, he realised that some family must be grieving over the death of the young man. He therefore ordered his soldiers to hang the headless corpse on the walls of the palace and to arrest anyone seen weeping before it.

When the dead thief's mother came to hear of this, she pleaded with her son to recover his brother's body. "I beg of you, he must be buried with the proper ceremonies. If not, he will surely wander the land as a ghost for all eternity. If you will not go to the pharaoh, I shall beseech him on my knees. At worst, I shall bury you and your brother in peace beside your father."

Nothing the other brother said could change her mind. But rather than confess to the pharaoh, he decided to try and steal the body.

Pretending to be a foolish and absent-minded wine merchant, he drove two donkeys past the soldiers who were guarding his brother's corpse. Each donkey was laden down with goat skins full of strong red wine. Driving the donkeys on with a good strong stick, he hurried them forward. In their haste to escape a beating, the donkeys collided with each other and several of the goat-skin bags fell to the ground and burst open.

The soldiers rushed to his aid, not so much to help such a foolish man but in their desire to make sure that as little as possible of the good red wine would seep into the sand. As they expected, the wine-merchant invited them to help themselves, first to the wine that would otherwise have seeped away and then to share another goat-skin bag or two ... or three! By the time night fell all the soldiers were sprawled on the ground in drunken sleep.

The pharaoh was furious when he was told that the headless corpse had mysteriously disappeared from the palace walls. But he was a cunning man and determined to outwit the thief. He made it known that he would give his daughter in marriage to the man who could tell her the cleverest and most wicked trick in all Egypt. The treasure thief understood at once what was behind the pharaoh's plan but by now he was determined to outfox the pharaoh in every move he made.

In the dusk of evening he came to the palace and asked to speak with the princess. Under his cloak he carried his dead brother's arm (ugh!). In the dark gloom of her chamber, the princess listened in disbelief as the thief told how he and his brother had been caught in the trap, how he had slain his brother, and then how he had stolen his brother's corpse under the very noses of the pharaoh's soldiers.

"Surely no one has told so clever and wicked a tale."

But the princess grabbed his arm. "Guards! Guards! Come quickly. The mystery is solved. I have the thief by the arm!"

Indeed she had the thief by the arm, but it was the arm of the dead one! His brother had slipped out through the window in the darkness.

Well, when Rameses III heard of this latest feat, he could not believe that anyone could be so clever and so daring. Rather than have such a cunning enemy he proclaimed that the thief would be pardoned if he came forward and vowed to serve the pharaoh faithfully and for ever.

So, in the end, the treasure thief married the daughter of Rameses III. He became the pharaoh's loyal servant and never again did he have any need to make use of the secret passage built by his father, the master-builder.

AMAZING!

There you are, hands tied behind your back, blindfolded — and alone in a dark, musty maze — deep in an old Egyptian tomb. Caught unawares when the accomplice of the spy you'd been shadowing, pounced on you from behind, there had been nothing you could do.

"We'll be well out of the country by the time you find your way out of here," they'd sneered as they left, "should take you at least three hours ..."

But it doesn't. You stumble out into daylight and into the arms of a surprised caretaker within an hour. How do you do it?

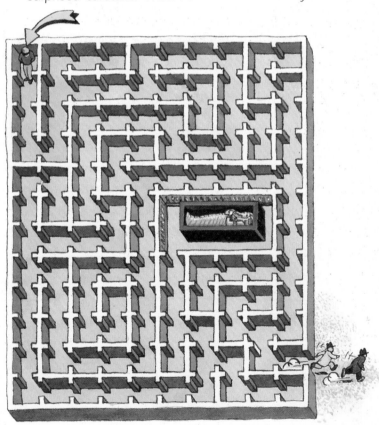

Remember this trick which works for most mazes. Put your right elbow on a wall and start walking. By keeping it on the wall at all times, you must eventually come to the entrance. It's a long walk, but that way, you don't double back on your tracks ... and there's time to catch the spies at the airport!

CLEOPATRA
– mystery lady of the Nile?

WHO WAS SHE?

Cleopatra was born in ancient Egypt in 69 BC. Following the customs of the day, she married her youngest brother Ptolemy XIII. (Imagine having to marry your brother!) Together they became King and Queen of Egypt, when Cleopatra was only eighteen years old. It wasn't a happy marriage. They squabbled and by the time Julius Caesar arrived on the scene from Rome, Cleopatra had been deprived of power altogether.

Julius Caesar fell in love with Cleopatra, and with the might of his army behind him, he recaptured Egypt's throne for her. Ptolemy was killed in a battle not long after, and Cleopatra had to share the throne again with her thirteen-year-old brother. (Yes, husband number two, called Ptolemy XIV)

In 44 BC, Caesar was murdered and another powerful Roman called Mark Anthony now held Cleopatra's fate in his hands. He too fell for Cleopatra's charms and for twelve years he cared for her and Egypt's throne. Poor Ptolemy XIV was poisoned.

In 31 BC, Mark Anthony was defeated in battle by a new powerful Roman called Octavian, and so killed himself. And Cleopatra? It appears Octavian was not charmed by her, and so she too, chose to kill herself.

HOW SHOULD WE REMEMBER CLEOPATRA?

Cleopatra was not the mysterious beauty our modern movie producers would have us believe. On Egyptian coins of the time, she appears rather plain, with a strong hooked nose. However, it seems she had a powerful and charming personality. She could speak six languages and had a good knowledge of history and philosophy. But more importantly, she was a skilful, ambitious ruler who succeeded in a world dominated by men. In today's world, she might have made an excellent politician, although perhaps a rather ruthless one . . .!

Three of the world's

The Pyramid of Cheops

This enormous pyramid sometimes called The Great Pyramid, is 137 metres high and was built about 4,500 years ago by an Egyptian pharaoh called Cheops, also known as Khufu. No one knows why he built it. Some people say he was so conceited that he just wanted to keep his name alive, others say it is a huge calendar or astronomical calculator. However, the world's archeologists, scientists and engineers cannot come up with an answer. Neither do they know how the labourers managed to lift stones that weighed up to 2.5 tonnes without the help of modern machinery. It is believed to have taken about 20 years to complete. It may have been built by farmers who could not farm their land during the yearly floods.

Stonehenge

This great ring of stones on Salisbury Plain in Wiltshire was probably built in 2200 BC. The main part is a huge circle of standing stones with flat stones laid across the top of them. Inside this circle is another ring of smaller stones with a large block in the centre. No one knows if it was designed for religious ceremonies or as an observatory. If it was some kind of giant

unsolved mysteries

calendar, it is amazing that they managed to work out the positions of the sun and moon so accurately that they could line up the stones in precisely the right positions. Some of the huge 35 tonne stones were transported from as far as 36 km away. Later, in 1600 BC some giant bluestones from the Prescelly Mountains 225 km away were set up beside those already there. These enormous stone blocks were probably moved by dragging them on rollers but it must have taken a very long time. The reason why it was built still remains a mystery.

Sacsahuaman

Sacsahuaman is a stone fortress that stands high in the Andes Mountains, above the city of Cuzco in Peru, South America. The main part of Cuzco where only the Emperor, nobles and their servants were allowed to live, was built between two small rivers. The Incas believed this was the centre of the world. They laid the city out in the shape of a puma; some of them believed this animal was a god. Sacsahuaman, the fortress, was the puma's head. It was built without cement or mortar and is still standing. It is difficult to imagine how the Incas managed to shape the 20 tonne stones so that they would fit closely together, and also how they moved them. For the Incas had no horses, oxen or iron tools, nor had they yet discovered the wheel.

King Solomon
and the Queen of Sheba
— a royal mystery

The bright sun shines hot on the throngs lining the streets of ancient Jerusalem. People in the crowd elbow and jostle each other, standing tiptoe, craning to snatch a glimpse of the splendid procession.

There are hundreds of camels, each magnificiently groomed and draped in beautifully patterned rugs. Their gold and silver harnesses sparkle in the sunlight. There are court officials, nobles of different rank, servants and ladies-in-waiting. Two long lines of fierce-looking warriors flank the procession, shielding it from the crowds of milling citizens. And the sounds of music rise above the general din, adding to the clamour and excitement.

But the focus of attention is the ornate sedan chair, moving sedately forward on the broad shoulders of six muscular bearers. Behind the fine silk screen, a tall stately figure can be seen. A golden tiara studded with gems and precious stones. The glint of gold from bracelets and necklaces. This is the woman all Jerusalem has been waiting to see: the mysterious Bilqîs, Queen of Sheba. She has come to exchange gifts with King Solomon, the wise ruler of Israel.

The only historical record we have of this occasion is a very brief mention in the Bible. It simply states that the Queen of Sheba came to visit King Solomon and gave him gifts of gold, silver, spices and precious stones.

But the event has been celebrated in story and song for 3000 years. It is said that Solomon fell hopelessly in love with this mysterious Queen. Exactly who she was and precisely where Sheba was located, remain mysteries to this day.

Some say that Bilqîs was from Africa, that she married King Solomon and that their son was the first in a line of kings who ruled Ethiopia down to 1974. In that year, their direct descendant, Emperor Haile Selassie, was overthrown.

Others believe that Sheba was located at the tip of the Arabian pennisula, roughly where Yemen is today.

Mystery surrounds King Solomon too. He was fabulously wealthy. He is believed to have had gold mines which were rich beyond belief. The Bible mentions those mines which were at a place called Ophir. But to the frustration of generations of adventurers, the Bible does not tell *where* Ophir was.

The search for King Solomon's mines has taken people to Africa and many other parts of the world. The Spanish, for example, when they saw the great quantities of gold and silver possessed by the Incas and the Aztecs, wondered whether King Solomon's mines might not have been located in South America. But recent work by geologists suggest that Ophir was in an area between Medina and Mecca on the Arabian penninsula.

The mystery remains . . .

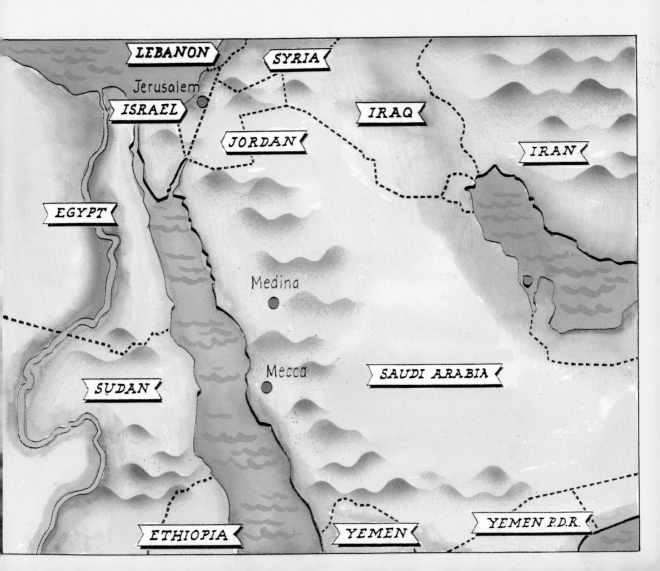

THE SHROUD OF TURIN

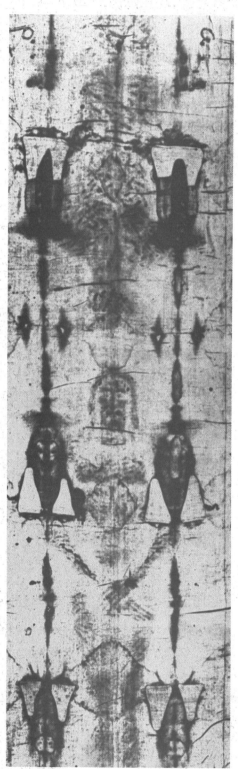

For hundreds, if not thousands of years, people have wrapped corpses in pieces of cloth ready for burial. The cloth is usually known as a shroud. The shroud of Turin is special because millions of people have believed it was used to cover the dead body of Jesus Christ.

On the 4.5 metre-long cloth, you can see what looks like the imprint of a man. It is almost like an x-ray or photograph. It is said that you can see where perhaps the crown of thorns encircled the head, causing cuts and bleeding. Other wounds can be seen too, in the ribs and arms. The man is bearded and looks like Christ is supposed to have looked. It is very unusual for any likeness at all to be imprinted on a shroud.

The shroud was first displayed in public in 1357, in a small French town. No one can explain exactly how it came to be in the hands of the de Charny family. In 1578 it was taken to Turin cathedral in Italy.

Recently tests have been carried out on tiny samples of the shroud, in order to work out the age of the cloth. The results indicated that the cloth is almost definitely from the thirteenth or fourteenth centuries, and so it cannot have been Jesus Christ's shroud. However, the mystery of how the blood-stained image of a crucified man appeared on the cloth is still unsolved, and the church believes that the shroud will still be an object of veneration.

IL VERISSIMO RITRATTO DEL SANTISSIMO SVDARIO
DEL NOSTRO SALVATORE GIESV CHRISTO

How was the shroud so draped over the corpse that
both front and back images appear? Here is one possible
explanation, conceived by the 16th-century painter
Giorgio Giulio Clovio.

SPECIAL DAYS
GOOD FRIDAY

WHAT DOES GOOD FRIDAY COMMEMORATE?

It's the anniversary of the crucifixion of Jesus Christ and always marks the beginning of Easter, although the special days of Ash Wednesday (first day of Lent), Palm Sunday (first day of Holy Week) and Maundy Thursday (anniversary of the night of the Last Supper) are celebrated first.

WHERE DOES ITS NAME COME FROM?

It sounds strange, doesn't it, to call a solemn day, the saddest day for Christians, Good Friday? Scholars believe that it was either once named God's Friday, or else that the "Good" simply meant holy. The Anglo-Saxons used to call it Long Friday (because the church services were so long) and in the Greek Church it was often described as Great Friday. Germans also had two names for this special day. One was Karfreitag (sad or sorrowful Friday), the other Stille Freitag (Silent Friday).

HOW IS IT CELEBRATED?

Once it was strictly a day for fasting and repenting of sins. People dressed in black. Church altars were bare. No bells tolled, no organs pealed. Because Christ was nailed to the cross, blacksmiths refused to shoe horses, no one used a hammer and churchgoers walked barefoot to church for fear the nails in their shoes would leave marks on the ground. There was no ploughing, no clothes were washed and no graves were dug.

60

Many superstitions sprang up, especially around the idea that on this one day, Satan had no power over earth. So it became a lucky day to be born (these children had "second sight", people said, meaning they believed they could see into the future). It was also lucky to plant crops, particularly potatoes.

Most of the customs have died out, but we've kept the one of eating hot cross buns (even though this probably goes back to pagan times). Once these had to be baked fresh on Good Friday morning and each year every household saved at least one Easter bun or loaf, partly for luck, but partly because it was believed these had the power of healing. Scrapings from the bun were stirred into water and drunk as a cure for everything from flu to warts.

Nowadays, Good Friday is still one of the most important days in the Christian Church's calendar and is celebrated as a day of solemn mourning and remembrance.

EASTER DAY

Easter Day is the opposite of Good Friday: on this day, Christians unite in feelings of joy as they celebrate Christ's resurrection. Churches are massed with white flowers as a symbol of purity and bells ring out to proclaim the resurrection of Christ. Over the years the custom of wearing new clothes to church developed and an old English rhyme warned — At Easter let your clothes be new, or else be sure you will it rue. It's thought Easter bonnet parades might have come from this.

THE LORD OF THE DANCE

I Danced in the morning
when the world was begun,
and I danced in the moon
and the stars and the sun,
and I came down from heaven
and I danced on the earth,
at Bethlehem I had my birth.

(Chorus):

Dance, then wherever you may be,
I am the Lord of the Dance, said he.
And I'll lead you all wherever you may be,
and I'll lead you all in the dance, said he.

I Danced for the scribe
and the pharisee,
but they would not dance
and they wouldn't follow me.
I danced for the fishermen,
for James and John;
they came with me
and the dance went on.

(Chorus)

62

I Danced on the Sabbath
and I cured the lame.
The holy people they
said it was a shame.
They whipped and they stripped
and they hung me on high,
and they left me there
on the cross to die.

(*Chorus*)

I Danced on a Friday
when the sky turned black.
It's hard to dance
with the devil on your back.
They buried my body
and they thought I'd gone
but I am the dance
and I still go on.

(*Chorus*)

They cut me down
and I leapt up high
I am the life
that'll never, never die.
I'll live in you
if you'll live in me.
I am the Lord
of the Dance, said he.

(*Chorus*)

Sydney Carter

THE PHANTOM HOUND OF YORKSHIRE

Was it real creature — or a phantom hound of heaven? The Reverend Isaac Woodcock was never sure . . .

Mr Woodcock lived in Yorkshire, England, over a hundred years ago. He had a number of parishes and often had to travel by horseback or on foot over the open countryside. Sometimes he carried large amounts of money, collections from different churches to help support missions and take care of poor people.

The area where the clergyman lived was notorious for thieves and murderers, who preyed on the weak and helpless. But the Reverend Isaac Woodcock was neither weak nor helpless. He was not afraid of the men he called "the wicked doers of the devil's work," although many people thought he should be.

The night of February 6, 1854, seemed to be made for "the devil's work." It was bitterly cold and windy. Thick clouds rode the sky, and the pale moon shone fitfully.

On this winter's night, the good Mr Woodcock was taking home two large sacks. One held important papers; the other held a large amount of money. He had strung the sacks across his shoulders by a heavy cord, and they bounced against his sides as he walked.

He was not armed. He was well protected, he said, "by the Good Book I carry with me everywhere". He kept it handy in his coat pocket.

As the fearless clergyman walked along the dark road, he quoted biblical verses to himself. It made the time pass

more easily. A light snow began to fall. In the cloudy light, the silvery snow gave an eerie glow to the trees and shrubs on both sides of the road.

Mr Woodcock heard an owl hoot close by. A moment later, the voice of another owl answered from deep in the surrounding woods. "At least," the clergyman told himself, "I think those are owls I hear".

Just then the clouds parted, and the landscape was bathed in brilliant moonlight. This was followed by a few seconds of silence. It was finally broken by the steady beat of footsteps. They were coming from somewhere behind the clergyman. The footsteps came faster and faster, closer and closer.

Mr Woodcock stopped and wheeled around. "Who is there?" he called out.

And from out of a thin mist swirling behind him, a giant hound padded into the moonlight. It had a thick, uncombed coat of grey fur. It stood about level with the clergyman's chest, and he was a man about two metres tall. But what captured his attention was the huge creature's eyes. They glowed with what he called "a white fire," like two small moons under a thin film of clouds.

This strange animal padded right up to the clergyman, but Mr Woodcock was unafraid. He put out his hand to the dog, and the animal showed only friendliness. The large, rough tongue licked one of the clergyman's hands. At the same time, the dog turned its weird eyes up to stare at the man. They looked at each other for a long moment. Then, as if by agreement, they began to walk along the road. The dog stayed just to the right of the good man, never falling behind or going ahead.

Less than fifteen minutes passed, when the dog's behaviour suddenly changed. It moved into the lead by several metres. Then, looking back as if to check on the clergyman's safety, it left the road and trotted along the shadowy line of trees.

All of a sudden the dog was gone, swallowed by the trees and darkness. Mr Woodcock came to a halt, listening. There was no sound at all — not even the normal whistles and snapping twigs and other night sounds of birds and animals that are active in the dark hours. "It was a most unnatural silence," the clergyman said later. "It was as if I had entered another world."

Then the dog reappeared. Moving low to the ground, it came out of the woods and right up to the man. But it suddenly whirled toward the woods again and began to growl, a deep rumbling in its thick chest.

Now the clergyman heard a new sound. It was a brushing sound, such as clothing makes when it rubs against brush and branches. He turned in the direction it came from. As he did so, he caught a glimpse of three men slipping in and out of the shadows. The dog seemed rooted where it stood. It continued to growl menacingly at the spot where those men had been.

Mr Woodcock patted the dog and started walking along the road again. It was growing late. His family would soon begin to worry about him. He didn't want them wandering about on a night like this, hunting for him.

Man and dog had travelled no more than another hundred metres when the deep growls started again. Again Mr Woodcock searched in the direction the dog was facing. The moon was out now, and he saw, outlined against the sky, the same three men. They had come out of the woods and were standing farther down the road, waiting.

The dog leapt into a run, directly for the men. They broke for the cover of the trees. Soon the clergyman could hear branches cracking as they plunged deeper into the woods.

Mr Woodcock caught up with the dog. "The quicker we get away from this place, the better," he said to his furry companion. And he set off at a good pace, the dog trotting alongside.

The would-be thieves were seen three more times by the clergyman as he made his way along the wooded path. Each time they seemed about to come at him. And one time he thought he saw weapons — guns and knives — in their hands. But each time they came out of hiding they were frightened off by Mr Woodcock's growling guardian.

"However much they wanted the money at my side," the clergyman

remarked, "they were not willing to risk the fury of my companion to come after it".

At long last, the walk ended as the clergyman reached his home. Standing just a few metres from the front door, Mr Woodcock beckoned to the dog to come inside. "I will feed you," the man said.

The dog moved close to the clergyman. He licked the man's hand just the way he had before. He gazed at the man with those twin-moon eyes, barked softly one time — and vanished.

The Reverend Isaac Woodcock told the events of that fantastic night again and again, until the end of his life. He believed firmly that it had all happened just the way he remembered it. He talked to everyone who lived within several kilometres of his home, asking about the phantom of the night. Nobody knew of such an animal. Not one person had ever seen or heard about a dog anything like that one.

They were sure that the clergyman's life — and the church's money — had been saved that night by a supernatural creature. In time, the clergyman came to share their feelings. And every time he walked the road that wound through the dark woods, he kept a sharp lookout for his phantom friend. The dog never reappeared. But then, Mr Woodcock was never again followed by thieves!

Written by Louis Sabin
Illustrated by Rachel Legge

Tell me

The ghosts of my life
are the people I knew,
the people who've long since gone.
For I left them behind,
those people I loved,
as I grew and I travelled on.

And now while I wait
my memories grow
and I ask the question once more:
Will those people I knew
be waiting for me
on the other side of that door?

Wendy Body

They shut the road through the woods
Seventy years ago.
Weather and rain have undone it again,
And now you would never know
There was once a road through the woods
Before they planted the trees.
It is underneath the coppice and heath,
And the thin anemones.
Only the keeper sees
That, where the ring-dove broods,
And the badgers roll at ease,
There was once a road through the woods.

The

Way

Through

the

Woods

Yet, if you enter the woods
Of a summer evening late,
When the night-air cools on the trout-ringed pools
Where the otter whistles his mate
(They fear not men in the woods,
Because they see so few),
You will hear the beat of a horse's feet,
And the swish of a skirt in the dew,
Steadily cantering through
The misty solitudes,
As though they perfectly knew
The old lost road through the woods . . .
But there is no road through the woods!

Rudyard Kipling

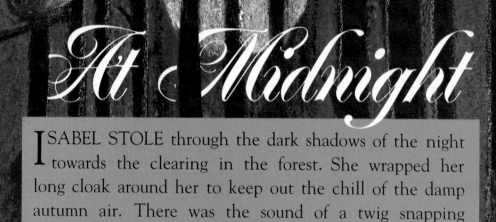

At Midnight

ISABEL STOLE through the dark shadows of the night towards the clearing in the forest. She wrapped her long cloak around her to keep out the chill of the damp autumn air. There was the sound of a twig snapping behind her. Shuddering, Isabel pressed her body against a thick tree trunk and waited. The forest was quiet. The whole world seemed silent, waiting, like Isabel.

Her mind fled back to the dangerous moments when she had crept out of her father's house. A tall oak tree grew close to her upstairs window. She had climbed onto one of its strong branches and then slipped down from one branch to another, past her father's bedroom window and to the ground. A candle had glowed in the room, casting light on his sleeping face. Then it had sputtered out.

Now Isabel began to run again to the place in the forest where she always met Thomas. She wanted to arrive first tonight, to watch him ride up on his black horse, the two of them trembling with exhaustion. If all went well, he would be there within the quarter hour. If all went well. . . .

The cold fingers of fear crept around Isabel's mind. She loved a highwayman, a robber who stopped the rich at night in their coaches and stole from them. Thomas only took money from those who had too much; he was a kind and gentle man who never passed a beggar by. But he had a wild nature that showed in his dark eyes. Isabel feared that one night Thomas would meet death instead of her. She also feared her father, who had forbade her ever to see Thomas again.

Isabel pushed aside a low branch and stepped into the clearing. The moonlight shone down through the open space in the canopy of trees overhead. A horse snorted. Isabel's heart jumped, and she whirled around.

Bushes rustled, then a black horse stepped out into the clearing. Thomas's laughter shattered the stillness. He reached down his arms, caught up Isabel, and set her on the horse in front of him.

"I have something to tell you, sweet Isabel," he said. "Tonight was my last night as a highwayman."

Isabel turned to look with wide eyes into his face.

"Tomorrow night," he said, "I'll take you away with me and make you my wife. We'll have a new life, far from your father and far from my past."

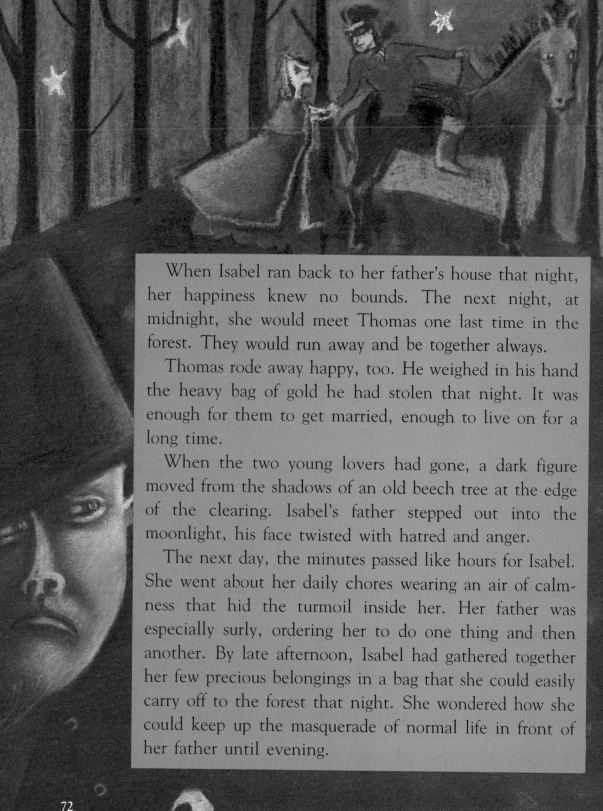

When Isabel ran back to her father's house that night, her happiness knew no bounds. The next night, at midnight, she would meet Thomas one last time in the forest. They would run away and be together always.

Thomas rode away happy, too. He weighed in his hand the heavy bag of gold he had stolen that night. It was enough for them to get married, enough to live on for a long time.

When the two young lovers had gone, a dark figure moved from the shadows of an old beech tree at the edge of the clearing. Isabel's father stepped out into the moonlight, his face twisted with hatred and anger.

The next day, the minutes passed like hours for Isabel. She went about her daily chores wearing an air of calmness that hid the turmoil inside her. Her father was especially surly, ordering her to do one thing and then another. By late afternoon, Isabel had gathered together her few precious belongings in a bag that she could easily carry off to the forest that night. She wondered how she could keep up the masquerade of normal life in front of her father until evening.

She did not have to. An hour before suppertime, her Aunt Charlotte rode up to their house in her carriage.

"Isabel, go pack a bag," her father demanded when her aunt came into the house. "You are going home with your aunt. She will keep you for several days."

"But, Father—" she began.

Then she met his eyes and saw the steely, hard look in them. Somehow, he knew.

Hot blood flushed her face; she ran to her bedroom. Quickly she gathered together her bag and another satchel of clothes. She would go with her aunt. But then she would escape and run to the forest, even though it was farther from her aunt's house than her own. She would still meet Thomas, as she had promised, at midnight.

"Hurry now," her father told them as they stepped into the carriage. "Night will fall soon. And the highwaymen will foul the countryside with their thievery."

Isabel avoided her father's face as the carriage jolted forward and then sped away from his house. Her aunt leaned close to her.

"If you try to run away, Isabel," she said, "I will call the sheriff. Your father has told me what to say."

Isabel squeezed her eyes shut to keep the tears from welling up. Her father had thought of everything. If she tried to escape, he would send the sheriff after her. And if the sheriff found Thomas . . .

All through dinner and the long evening at her aunt's house, Isabel kept her composure. But her mind was frantic, devising and then casting away and then revising

plans for escape. Finally, at ten o'clock, her aunt led her to a bedroom.

"Go to sleep, Isabel," she said in a firm voice. "But do not try to escape. I will be sitting outside the door."

Isabel gently kissed her aunt on the cheek but did not meet her eyes. She shut the heavy door to the room and latched it. First she went to the windows. She tried to push up on the sashes. Then she saw how strong her prison was. New nails had been pounded into the frames and the sill. She would never be able to open them. And even if she could shatter the glass without her aunt hearing, the panes were too small for her to climb through. Isabel fell onto the bed and wept. Thomas would be waiting for her in two hours.

Isabel woke with a start. Frantically she looked around the room for a clock. She had cried herself asleep. Now it was midnight. The horrible dream came back. She had been dreaming about Thomas. He had called to her, a terrible scream that had awakened her.

Isabel crept from the bed and slowly opened the door. A chair was sitting in the hallway, but her aunt had left. She threw her cloak around her, tied a warm woollen scarf around her neck, and picked up her bag of belongings. Thomas would still be waiting for her; she was sure.

A short time later Isabel was running through the night toward the clearing in the woods.

Her face was streaked with tears and scratches by the time she reached the clearing. She had run wildly for almost an hour, her heart full of foreboding and fear.

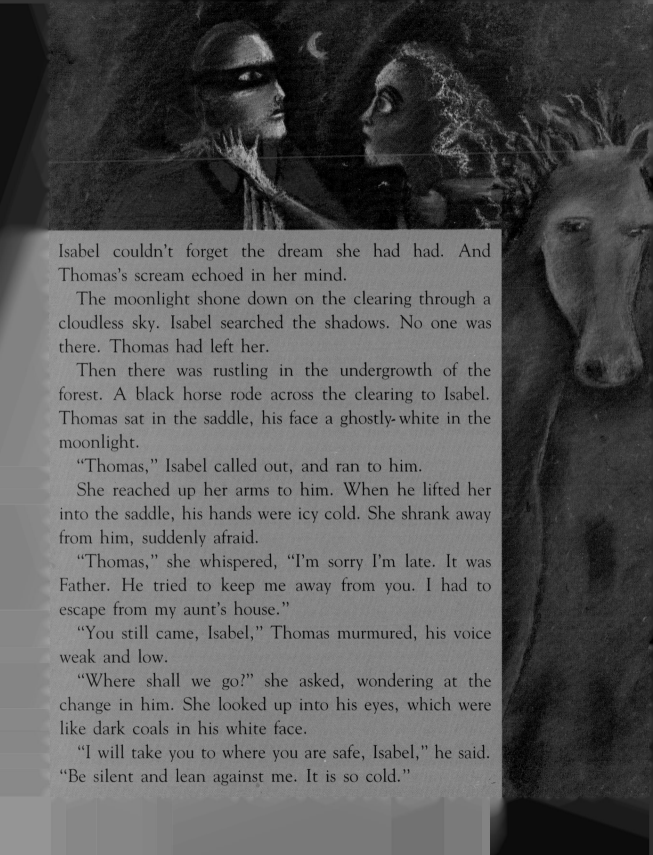

Isabel couldn't forget the dream she had had. And Thomas's scream echoed in her mind.

The moonlight shone down on the clearing through a cloudless sky. Isabel searched the shadows. No one was there. Thomas had left her.

Then there was rustling in the undergrowth of the forest. A black horse rode across the clearing to Isabel. Thomas sat in the saddle, his face a ghostly-white in the moonlight.

"Thomas," Isabel called out, and ran to him.

She reached up her arms to him. When he lifted her into the saddle, his hands were icy cold. She shrank away from him, suddenly afraid.

"Thomas," she whispered, "I'm sorry I'm late. It was Father. He tried to keep me away from you. I had to escape from my aunt's house."

"You still came, Isabel," Thomas murmured, his voice weak and low.

"Where shall we go?" she asked, wondering at the change in him. She looked up into his eyes, which were like dark coals in his white face.

"I will take you to where you are safe, Isabel," he said. "Be silent and lean against me. It is so cold."

Isabel pulled off her soft woollen scarf.

"Wear this, Thomas," she said, and lovingly wrapped it around his neck.

Thomas kissed Isabel on the top of her head; they rode in silence through the dark woods.

Isabel shut her eyes and leaned her head into her lover's chest. She could feel the warmth of her slowly work its way into his heart.

Suddenly the horse stopped. Isabel opened her eyes and saw her aunt's house in front of them.

She looked at Thomas in confusion.

"Good-bye, Isabel," he said, helping her slip to the ground. "Good-bye, my love." Then he leaned down to kiss her.

Isabel shuddered when she felt his cold lips upon hers. She touched his cheek with her hand, staring into his deep eyes. She cried when he rode away into the blackness of the night.

Isabel awoke from a nightmare the next morning. It was Thomas's scream again, calling her name. Her aunt walked into the bedroom, carrying a breakfast tray.

"What is it, child?" she asked.

"Thomas," Isabel whispered. "Why did he leave me last night?"

"Then you know . . ." her aunt said with downcast eyes.

"Know?" Isabel said. Fear welled up in her chest.

"Thomas was hanged by the sheriff at midnight," her aunt said. "He will be buried this morning."

"No!" Isabel gasped. "It isn't true. I met him last night in the forest. It was after midnight. But he had waited. He brought me back here on his horse."

"No, Isabel. That was a dream. Thomas was dead at midnight."

Isabel jumped from the bed and hurriedly dressed.

"Why do you say he is dead? If he is dead, where is his body?"

"In the church crypt," her aunt answered. "But you mustn't go."

Isabel ran from the room and out the door of the house. The Church was not far; she ran until her breath tore at her chest. The priest was standing at the doors of the church.

"Thomas!" she cried out to the priest. "It can't be true."

The priest's eyes were full of pity. Isabel rushed past him and down the stairs to the crypt of the church. There, lying in a wood coffin, was Thomas.

Isabel walked slowly toward him. His face was ghostly white, as it had been the night before. His dark eyes were closed forever. And around his neck was the soft, woollen scarf she had put there, to keep her love warm.

Written by J. B. Stamper
Illustrated by Judy Byford

77

Leeds, capital of Yorkshire, is one of the largest cities in England. Situated on the edge of the Pennines, it is an important industrial and cultural centre.

IT'S MY HOME **LEEDS**

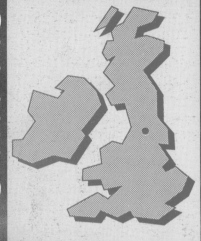

Leeds City Hall

1 Kirkstall Abbey
2 Leeds & Liverpool Canal
3 Armley Mills
4 Middleton Railway
5 Leeds City Centre
6 Temple Newsam Estate
7 Elland Road Stadium
8 Headingley Cricket Ground
9 International Swimming Pool

FROM its very beginning, Leeds has been a trading centre. In the twelfth century, Cistercian monks settled in the Aire valley and built Kirkstall Abbey. They introduced spinning, weaving and pottery to the area. Leeds developed as a market town for their products.

There was a good supply of wool from sheep kept on the Pennine hills, and over the centuries Leeds became a very important centre for the production of woollen cloth.

Towards the end of the eighteenth century the Middleton Railway was built, to bring coal in from the coalfield. At first the wagons of coal were pulled by horses, but in the early nineteenth century steam locomotives were developed and used.

The Leeds to Liverpool canal was also opened in the late eighteenth century. It provided a very important link with the port at Liverpool. As a result of the railway and the canal, industry grew a great deal. The Town Hall is one of several very impressive nineteenth century buildings which show how wealthy Leeds became.

The Leeds to Liverpool canal is still open today and is used for boating, angling and canoeing. The annual Trans Pennine Canal Marathon is a popular challenge for keen canoeists. Leeds United Football Club is based at Elland Road Stadium, and Yorkshire County Cricket Club has its home at Headingley Cricket Ground. Leeds International Pool held the first swimming marathon in the country in 1984 ☐

The Waratah mystery

It was only her second voyage. In 1909 the steamship *Waratah* was still new, still the pride of her line. She had been built especially for the Australian migrant trade and was expected to make many trips back and forth between England and Australia.

But fate decided otherwise.

On July 26th, her coalbunkers all refilled, her 10 000 tonnes of cargo safely stowed, the *Waratah* left the port of Durban in South Africa, and headed for London. On board were 211 passengers and crew.

The next day she overtook another ship, the *Clan McIntyre* in bad wather near Cape Agulhas. Then she vanished — completely!

At first, because the ship was not fitted with radio, she was not posted missing and people waited months, expecting her to limp into port with a story of engine breakdown or some other hold up.

"She can't have sunk," anxious friends and relatives told each other, "there's no sign of wreckage. Perhaps she lost power and is drifting far from the usual shipping lanes."

They raised money to charter a rescue ship and in February 1910, the *S. S. Wakefield* set off from Durban to search for the lost liner. She covered nearly 18 000 nautical miles, calling fruitlessly at many remote islands, hoping always to find at least one survivor. But there was nothing and nobody to be found anywhere.

A court of enquiry in England finally decided that as the ship was sound and the cargo properly loaded, the only possible conclusion was that the *Waratah* must have capsized in an exceptionally violent gale and gone down with all hands.

"But when ships sink," cried the relatives, "there's *always* wreckage. A floating life belt, fragments of decking, an empty lifeboat . . . Why was there nothing?"

No one could answer.

There are stories, of course. One tells of a passenger who left the ship in Durban because he kept dreaming of a corpse-like figure which warned him to leave the ship before it was too late. It says he also dreamed that the *Waratah* had capsized in a gale — long before people knew she was missing. Another tale says that an officer on the *S. S. Clan McIntyre* saw a strange old-fashioned sailing ship following the *Waratah*. Was it the ghostly *Flying Dutchman*, the phantom ship that brings disaster to sailors? Or was it just imagination?

No one can answer that either.

To this day, the fate of the *Waratah* remains a mystery.

The floating world of an
OCEAN LINER

Ocean liners have been described as floating resorts because of the many varied facilities on board. The diagram below is a cross section of the *Canberra* which cruises worldwide. Sometimes ocean liners are cruising for several weeks, and they have to provide everything the passengers need while they are at sea.

1 Bar	2 Theatre	3 Lounge	4 Restaurant	5 Club
6 Hairdressing Salon	7 Shop	8 Information Desk		9 Pool
10 Junior Club	11 Ocean Room	12 Restaurant		13 Island Room
14 Buffet	15 Library	16 Video and TV Room		17 Tavern
18 Gymnasium	19 Pool	20 Bar and Pool		21 Nightclub

ERIC NORTH

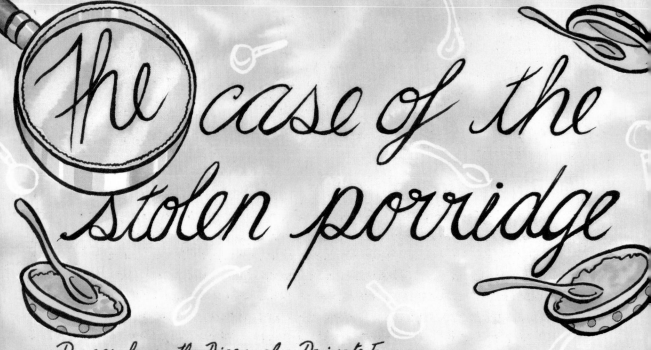

The case of the stolen porridge

Pages from the Diary of a Private Eye

Thursday 6 March

Dear Diary,

Well, it's nice to wrap up a case in just one day!

There I was quietly sitting at my desk, sipping my first cup of tea for the day when in walked this great, big bear with a story about a case of breaking and entering.

I asked him why he'd come to me and it turns out he felt the police weren't really interested in simple vandalism and theft. He's probably right. The papers are full of the murder of a big gambling boss called Cock Robin right now (apparently a sparrow confessed, but there's something fishy about it), so I guess the cops are pretty busy on that. Anyway, Father Bear said I'd been recommended to him by a relative who lived in the same woods as the Hood family and they'd been impressed by the way I'd tracked down that nasty character who was slinking around impersonating old ladies and grabbing little girls. (Nasty, the way he ate his victims.) I admitted it had been one of my brilliant efforts, especially acting the part of a woodcutter, which wasn't easy for a woman who's only 160 cm in her socks.

Thought for the day: Beware of wolves in grandmothers' clothing.

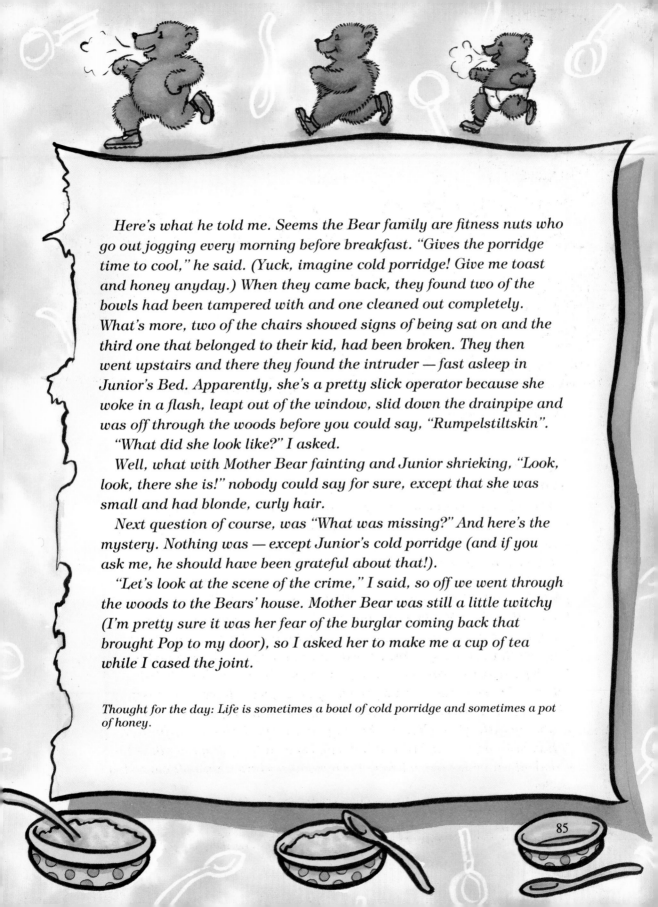

Here's what he told me. Seems the Bear family are fitness nuts who go out jogging every morning before breakfast. "Gives the porridge time to cool," he said. (Yuck, imagine cold porridge! Give me toast and honey anyday.) When they came back, they found two of the bowls had been tampered with and one cleaned out completely. What's more, two of the chairs showed signs of being sat on and the third one that belonged to their kid, had been broken. They then went upstairs and there they found the intruder — fast asleep in Junior's Bed. Apparently, she's a pretty slick operator because she woke in a flash, leapt out of the window, slid down the drainpipe and was off through the woods before you could say, "Rumpelstiltskin".

"What did she look like?" I asked.

Well, what with Mother Bear fainting and Junior shrieking, "Look, look, there she is!" nobody could say for sure, except that she was small and had blonde, curly hair.

Next question of course, was "What was missing?" And here's the mystery. Nothing was — except Junior's cold porridge (and if you ask me, he should have been grateful about that!).

"Let's look at the scene of the crime," I said, so off we went through the woods to the Bears' house. Mother Bear was still a little twitchy (I'm pretty sure it was her fear of the burglar coming back that brought Pop to my door), so I asked her to make me a cup of tea while I cased the joint.

Thought for the day: Life is sometimes a bowl of cold porridge and sometimes a pot of honey.

First I made this sketch of the downstairs room —

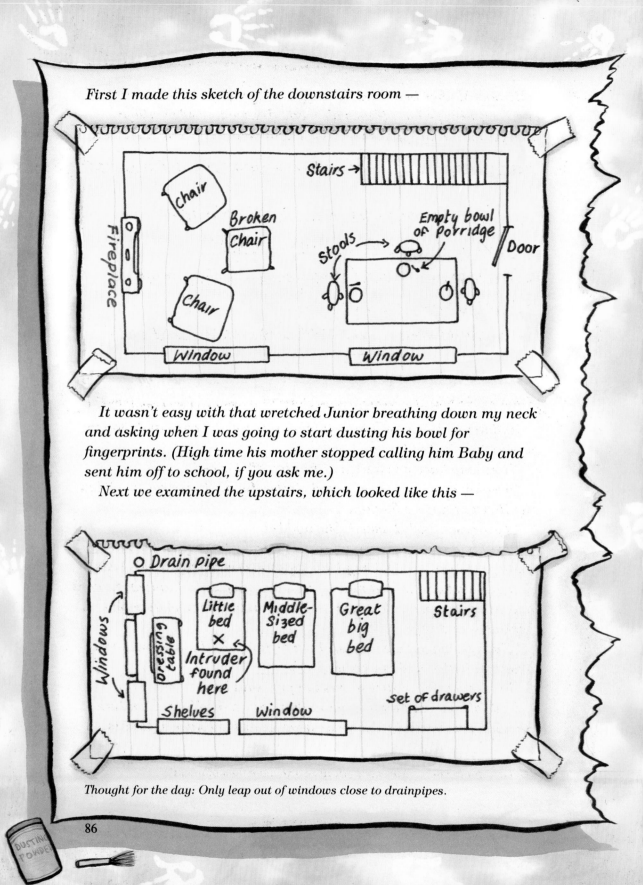

It wasn't easy with that wretched Junior breathing down my neck and asking when I was going to start dusting his bowl for fingerprints. (High time his mother stopped calling him Baby and sent him off to school, if you ask me.)

Next we examined the upstairs, which looked like this —

Thought for the day: Only leap out of windows close to drainpipes.

By now Mother Bear had the cuppa on the table and a nice batch of scones whipped up. (I was all ready to explain cold porridge brought me out in spots.) I sat down and made a note of the facts.

1/ The criminal was small, with blonde curly hair and was very athletic.
2/ Nothing was stolen (unless you count the porridge).
3/ One chair was broken.
4/ 2 chairs and 3 beds had been interfered with.

It didn't make sense. I had another scone with honey and thought it over. Suddenly I had an idea.

"How long have you had your furniture?" I asked.

"We only got it last week," said Mother Bear, "It was on special at the Heart Furniture Factory".

"Mattresses too?" I asked. She nodded.

Now I had it! I leapt to my feet, snatched a knife from the table and raced upstairs. Quickly I slit the mattress on Pop Bear's bed, plunged my hand in and pulled out a leather pouch. I untied the cord and turned it upside down. Out fell a sparkling heap of diamond necklaces and rings.

"The missing palace jewels," I said triumphantly," the ones every detective in the land is looking for!"

"No wonder the mattress was lumpy," said Pop.

Well, of course I had to explain that I knew the Heart Furniture Factory was owned by Jack Le Coeur, alias the Knave of Hearts.

Thought for the day: Hearts are always worth more than diamonds.

They'd kept it quiet that the jewels went missing the same day he made off with the tarts. (He's the black sheep of the family so it's a bit embarrassing for the King.) Jack had been picked up at the factory, but refused to tell where he'd hidden the jewels. He'd been locked away for a good long stretch for stealing and eating royal property, but all he had to do was sit tight till he came out. The police warned all us private eyes to keep our eyes skinned for the diamonds and that was that. Obviously, someone had worked out that Jack might have hidden the goods in a piece of furniture. And that someone had set out to do a spot of investigating. (I should have twigged it myself if I hadn't been so busy tracking down what happened to the Gingerbread kid.)

The rest was easy. There's only one criminal in these parts with a passion for cold porridge and that's Pol Flinders. She's fit as a flea, suffers from cold feet — and has inky black hair. I called round (with Pop Bear as bodyguard and witness) and there she was, sitting by the fire actually tucking into a bowl of the disgusting stuff.

"Thought it was time you met the gentleman whose house you broke into Pol," I said.

"You can't pin that on me," she gasped.

"Oh, no?" I said. "I've got three witnesses."

"But her hair's black," whispered Pop, "our burglar had golden curls".

"Haven't you heard of wigs, Pop?" I asked as I flung open a cupboard door.

And there, of course, was the blond wig.

Not that that was enough to convict her. But I'd also found a black hair on Junior's pillow that I was pretty sure would match one taken from Pol's head. I showed her and she realised the game was up.

Thought for the day: Many a blonde wig hides a brunette.

Seems she has a boyfriend who's a salesman for the Heart Factory and they'd come up with the idea that Jack must have hidden the jewels in one of the pieces of furniture. They'd checked all the items in stock and when that drew a blank, Pol had set out to track down all the furniture that had been sold recently, and that's what took her to the Bears' house. Where Pol went wrong was in presuming the goods must have been hidden inside a hollow arm or leg on a chair or bed. The mattress was just too obvious. Her big mistake was in falling asleep in Junior's bed so that the Bears could identify her, but then she'd been up all the night before, making that wig.

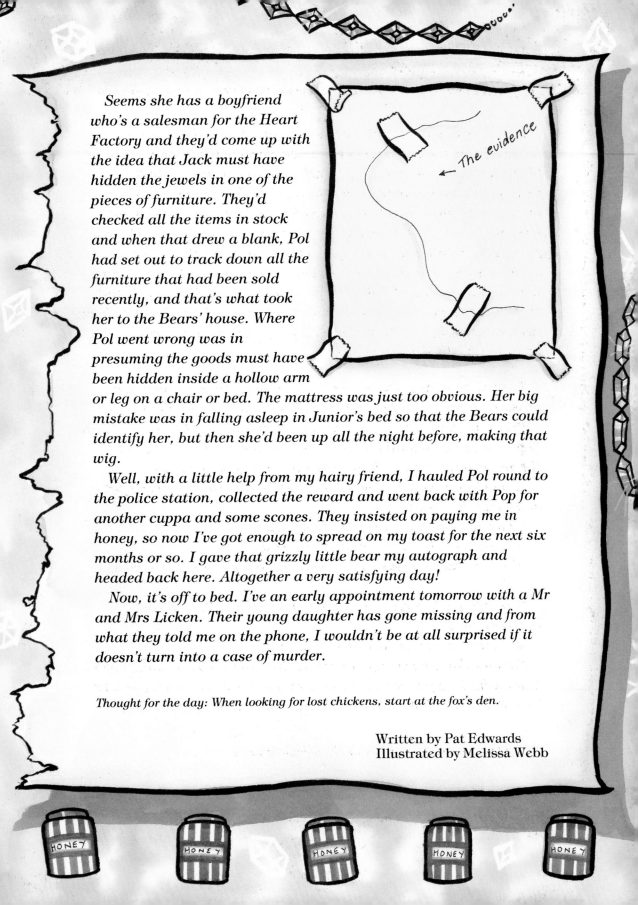

← The evidence

Well, with a little help from my hairy friend, I hauled Pol round to the police station, collected the reward and went back with Pop for another cuppa and some scones. They insisted on paying me in honey, so now I've got enough to spread on my toast for the next six months or so. I gave that grizzly little bear my autograph and headed back here. Altogether a very satisfying day!

Now, it's off to bed. I've an early appointment tomorrow with a Mr and Mrs Licken. Their young daughter has gone missing and from what they told me on the phone, I wouldn't be at all surprised if it doesn't turn into a case of murder.

Thought for the day: When looking for lost chickens, start at the fox's den.

Written by Pat Edwards
Illustrated by Melissa Webb

HONEY HONEY HONEY HONEY HONEY

IS YOUR ♥ IN

Imagine, you're walking through a graveyard in the dead of night. It's very still, very quiet. Suddenly behind you, a twig snaps. You hear heavy breathing. Panic strikes. You begin to run. Your heart starts pounding . . .

Calm down will ya

1 *Help! What's happening to my heart?* In the face of danger, fear causes remarkable things to happen in our bodies.

First of all, the body goes into a state of emergency and the brain instantly sends signals via the nervous system (they're like a network of wires) to two little emergency outposts in the body, called adrenal glands.

NERVOUS SYSTEM This Way →

2 The adrenal glands are perched like two small castles on top of the kidneys. On orders from the brain, the drawbridges are lowered and out pour hormones.

YOUR MOUTH?

3 Hormones are like juice. They flood into the blood-stream and rush straight to the heart, getting everything excited in their headlong rush.

Increase blood sugar!

Increase blood preasure.

Contract the blood vessels.

Pump faster.

Get out of the way.

4 The heart immediately responds!
- Blood sugar levels are boosted so you have lots of extra energy.
- Your heart beats faster so more oxygen is carried by the blood to the tissues. Now all your muscles can work extra well.
- The blood vessels narrow. Large amounts of blood are being forced through a smaller hole, causing higher blood pressure.

I'm trying! I'm trying!

5 And what does all this mean? In the face of danger it means you can either fight or flee, extra well or extra fast!

Stand and fight!

MOo!!

RUN!

91

HEARTY FACTS!

1 The heart is the most important muscle in the body. Like all muscles, it needs exercise.

2 The heart's job is to pump blood around the body, through the blood vessels or arteries.

Yes, alright!

Get a move on!

3 The blood vessels are part of the circulatory system and are like pathways around the body. They are an important link between the major organs and the limbs.

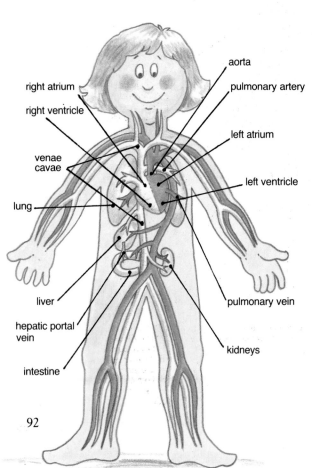

right atrium

right ventricle

venae cavae

lung

liver

hepatic portal vein

intestine

aorta

pulmonary artery

left atrium

left ventricle

pulmonary vein

kidneys

The main function of the circulatory system is to take fresh oxygen to the tissues, and to take carbon dioxide away.

Did you know that if you laid your blood vessels end to end they would encircle the world twice?

Did you know your heart isn't much bigger than a clenched fist? In an adult it pumps nearly 16,000 litres of blood through 95,000 km of blood vessels every day.

How your heart works

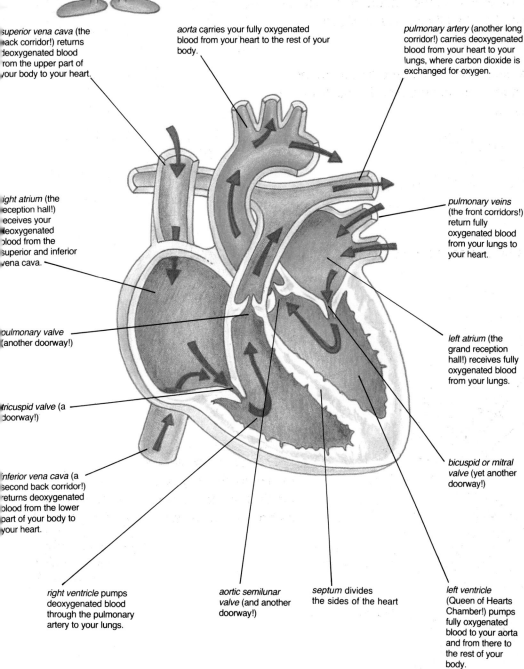

superior vena cava (the back corridor!) returns deoxygenated blood from the upper part of your body to your heart.

aorta carries your fully oxygenated blood from your heart to the rest of your body.

pulmonary artery (another long corridor!) carries deoxygenated blood from your heart to your lungs, where carbon dioxide is exchanged for oxygen.

right atrium (the reception hall!) receives your deoxygenated blood from the superior and inferior vena cava.

pulmonary veins (the front corridors!) return fully oxygenated blood from your lungs to your heart.

pulmonary valve (another doorway!)

left atrium (the grand reception hall!) receives fully oxygenated blood from your lungs.

tricuspid valve (a doorway!)

bicuspid or mitral valve (yet another doorway!)

inferior vena cava (a second back corridor!) returns deoxygenated blood from the lower part of your body to your heart.

right ventricle pumps deoxygenated blood through the pulmonary artery to your lungs.

aortic semilunar valve (and another doorway!)

septum divides the sides of the heart

left ventricle (Queen of Hearts Chamber!) pumps fully oxygenated blood to your aorta and from there to the rest of your body.

93

THE PHANTOM SAUSAGE STEALER!

Cast of characters (in order of appearance):

INTERCOM VOICE	VILLAIN	DELIVERY BOY	SERGEANT TREADHEAVY	W.P.C. GOLIGHTLY
	non-speaking role	a cheeky Cockney	a rotund policeman with delicate feet and red nose	a bubbly policewoman trying hard to be efficient
MRS PUGH frightfully lah-de-dah				

When staging this sketch, I suggest that the sausages be kept up the villain's sleeves by elastic bands.

The setting is a police station. W.P.C. Golightly is standing behind the counter combing her hair. The telephone rings and she answers it.

Golightly: Hello, Nutty Street Police Station. W.P.C. Golightly speaking . . . Who? . . . Oh, Sergant Treadheavy is in charge . . . Speak to him? No . . . er, yes. He's here . . . a-abouts.

(She covers the mouthpiece with her hand and looks off. The phone flex is fully extended and she struggles to get a better view.)

Oh, where is he? It's important. (She speaks into the phone again.)

Hold on. He's just coming.

(She gazes off-stage as if looking through a window and gives a running commentary on Sergeant Treadheavy's arrival.)

He's crossing the road. He's just coming. (To herself.) Come on . . . Over the zebra crossing and . . . oh, look out!

(We hear a crash from the wings and shouts of, 'Oy, oy, oy!')

(Sergeant Treadheavy makes a dramatic entrance seated in the basket of a Delivery Boy's bike. The Delivery Boy pulls up in front of the counter.)

Treadheavy: Oy, oy, oy! Why don't you ring your bell?

Boy: Because you're sitting on it.

Treadheavy: Get me out! Get me out!

(Golightly puts the phone on the counter and tries to pull him out. The Boy also helps but to no avail. Suddenly the Boy gets an idea. Golightly steadies the bike while the Boy lifts the back wheel so that the Sergeant as slowly tilted forward. He comes out with his feet on the floor but stays in a doubled-up position.)

Boy: Ha ha . . . a bent copper!

Sergeant Treadheavy: Ooh me back.

Golightly: Can't you straighten up?

Treadheavy: No it's me back, me back.

(Golightly cries to straighten him up, but the Boy again provides the solution.)

Boy: Try this.

(He pips the horn on his bike very loudly and the shock straightens up the Sergeant.)

Treadheavy: Ooh, that's better. Thank goodness (*He turns to the Boy*) Now then, my lad . . .

Golightly: Sergeant, quickly — the telephone. It's Scotland Yard.

Treadheavy: No, that's our telephone. They've got their own.

Golightly: No, they want to speak to you on it.

Treadheavy: Oh . . . eh? Scotland Yard? For me?

(*He picks up the phone. His helmet is askew and he inadvertently puts the earpiece to his helmet.*)

Hello? Hello?

(*He realises something is wrong. He puts the phone down, takes off his helmet with attention to the strap and places it over the phone. He looks round and now can't find the phone. He gets hold of the flex at the phone end and traces it to under his helmet. He then gets the handset through the strap and to his ear.*)

Hello. Yes. Who?

(*He looks overawed. He puts his helmet back on and salutes.*)

Yes, sir . . . Certainly, sir. Oh, I will, sir . . . Thank you, sir.

(*He salutes again and puts the phone down which pulls his helmet off. He replaces the handset, puts his helmet back on and walks back to the boy pulling the phone with him. He disentangles himself with Golightly's help, muttering "Scotland Yard" to himself until he is ready to face the Boy.*)

Treadheavy: Now then, let's deal with you, my lad. Hitting a police sergeant — an important police sergeant — with a bicycle on a zebra crossing is a serious offence. What's your name?

Boy: I've an excuse.

(*The Sergeant produces a pad and pencil and begins to write.*)

Treadheavy: Ivan . . . that's Russian, isn't it? E-X-C-U-S-E . . . excuse.

Golightly: That's not his name. This is the butcher's delivery boy, Philip Steak. I'm sure he didn't mean any harm.

Treadheavy: Mean any harm? I was halfway across the zebra crossing and he hit me right between the stripes.

Golightly: (*apologetically to the Boy*). That is serious.

Boy: Does it count if I hit him on a black square?

Treadheavy (*splutters*): What? Where do you think you were going at that speed?

Boy: I was in a hurry to get to the police station.

Treadheavy: Police station? Oh, well that's different. You'd better be going. Show him the way, Golightly.

Golightly: But he's here, Sergeant. This *is* the police station.

Treadheavy: Eh? Oh. Well, there you are then. There was no need for all that rush, was there? Now, what seems to be the trouble?

Boy: Somebody has taken my sausages.

Golightly: Sausages? (*She turns with alarm to the Sergeant.*)

Treadheavy: Sausages. (*He begins to write and then makes a sudden realisation.*) Sausages? That's what the phone call was about. Scotland Yard (*He salutes and then glares at Golightly till she salutes too.*) said they are looking for a phantom sausage stealer. They believe he's in our area and . . . (*He turns to the Boy.*) it appears you've found him.

Boy: No, he found me . . . and my sausages. Then he lost me.

Golightly: Did you get a good look at him?

Boy: Oh, yes. I chased him. He stole about five metres of sausages.
(*He goes into a mumbled description with action to show five metres, the thickness of the sausages and how they were knotted. Meanwhile, the Sergeant continues.*)

Treadheavy: Right, Golightly. Get on to the Pandas. It's not feeding time is it? (*He consults his watch.*) No. Get on to the Panda cars and tell 'em to look out for five metres of sausages . . . er . . . with a fella. Five metres O.K.?
(*Golightly goes to the intercom microphone and fiddles with it.*)

Boy: (*ends his mumbling*): . . . . five metres of sausages.

Treadheavy: Right, lad. Now give me a description.

Boy: Pardon?

Treadheavy: You know — size, colouring, etc.

Boy: Oh, well — very long, quite thin, er . . . pinkish colour . . . and knotted about every that much. (*He indicates about ten centimetres with his finger and thumb.*)

Treadheavy (*exasperated*): Not the sausages. The thief. What did he look like?

Boy: Let me think . . .

Golightly: Calling all cars, calling all cars. Be on the look-out for a string of sausages, last seen running down the High Street. Description to follow. (*She turns to listen to the Boy.*)

Boy (*to the Sergeant*):   Ah . . . short and thinnish.

Golightly (*over intercom*):   . . . They are short, thinnish sausages . . .

Boy: . . . with very big ears.

Golightly (*repeats without expression*):   . . . with big ears. (*To herself.*) Big ears? Could be, I suppose. Walls have ears.

Boy: And wearing a mask.

Golightly: And wearing a mask.

Intercom (*astonished*):   Sausages in masks?

Golightly: Yes. You've heard of bangers 'n' mashks. (*She grins and nods, then realises that she can't be right and frowns.*)

Treadheavy (*to Boy*):   Right. You get off down the High Street and see if you can find the man. Leave the rest to us.

Boy: Right. (*He wheels his bike towards the doors.*)

Golightly: Well, what do we do now?

Treadheavy: Well, when it strikes one, I has my lunch.
   (*We hear a gong-like bong.*)

Treadheavy: There it is.

Golightly: Wait a minute. It's only twenty past twelve.

Treadheavy: Then what was that we heard?

(*They both lean over the counter and look off-stage. Enter Mrs Pugh dragging a villainous-looking character. He is dressed in a sloppy sweater with very loose, dangly sleeves. Over his head is wedged a saucepan. Mrs Pugh leads him by the handle.*)

Mrs Pugh: Hello. My name's Mrs Pugh. Oh, **I am** glad I've found you. Look what I've found in one of my pans.

Treadheavy: What is it?

Mrs Pugh: It's a man!

Treadheavy: A man? In a pan? You can't cook a man in a pan. That must be against the law. I'll look it up in the book.

Mrs Pugh: I'm not going to cook him. Ugh, no! I've just found him. I opened my pantry and there he was.

Treadheavy: There who was?

Mrs Pugh: He was.

Treadheavy: Well?

Mrs Pugh: Well? Do something.

Treadheavy: What?

Mrs Pugh: Get him out. I want to use the pan. I want to cook my cabbage.

(*Golightly is examining the head under the pan.*)

Treadheavy: If you want to get the pan off, that's the fire-brigade, but if you want to get his head out, that's the hospital. Hospital for heads. Fire-brigade for pans.

Mrs Pugh: But . . . but I don't know who he is.

Treadheavy: Don't know who he is?

Mrs Pugh: No. I just found him in my pan.

Treadheavy: Well, that's not trespassing because he hasn't put his foot in it. We'll try breaking and entering. (*He consults a large book and mutters.*) Breaking and entering a saucepan . . .

Mrs Pugh: But I need my pan for my cabbage. What will I do if I can't do my cabbage?

Treadheavy: Couldn't you open a tin of peas?

Golightly: I think you should help, Sergeant. His head's quite stuck.

Treadheavy: You should have added a knob of butter. My mother always used to add a knob of butter. You don't get things sticking in your pans with butter.

Golightly (*knocks on the pan*): Can you hear me? Don't worry. We'll soon get you out. You're at the police station.

(*The pan becomes agitated.*)

Golightly: Oh, he's getting in a state. Don't worry. I'll hold your hand. Eeeeek!

Treadheavy: What's wrong?

Golightly: It's his hand. It's all cold and clammy.

(*She drops his hand on the counter. It is five sausages.*)

Treadheavy: It looks a bit pale. Here — let me rub it for you. (*He takes the hand, and as he shakes it the sausages come down the sleeve.*) By Jove! The missing links!

(*Mrs Pugh and Golightly discover that the other arm is the same.*)

Mrs Pugh: Ooh, it's horrible.

Treadheavy: Do you know, I bet this is our Phantom Sausage Stealer.

Golightly: Quick, Sergeant. Get the handcuffs.

(*The Sergeant searches his pockets. The Villain struggles and gets out of the pan. He has big false ears and a mask. He runs off with Treadheavy and Golightly in pursuit.*)

Mrs Pugh: It's my pan. It's my pan.

(*There are shouts off-stage. Treadheavy and Golightly run back across the stage followed by the Delivery Boy on his bike. This time the thief is in the basket. As they stop, Treadheavy and Golightly tie his feet and hands with sausages. He complains so they push one in his mouth as a gag.*)

Treadheavy: That's the end of a knotty problem.

(*A gong sounds off-stage.*)

Treadheavy: And there's the gong for lunchtime.

Golightly: But it's only half past twelve.

(*The gong continues. Enter Mrs Pugh with the pan on her head.*)

Treadheavy: I've told you before. Fire-brigade or hospital — or open a tin of peas.

(*Exit Mrs Pugh with the pan still on her head. The others follow.*)

CURTAIN

Written by Johnny Ball   Illustrated by Tim Lindsay

Not from the market, that's for sure!

Who was Circe? And why are her pigs important?

Circe was a beautiful and dangerous goddess, who lived on the island of Aeaea in the Mediterranean Sea. You can read about her in the famous book called *The Odyssey* by the ancient Greek poet Homer. The hero of the book is Odysseus, Lord of the Greek island of Ithaca. He is on his way home with his men after fighting for many years in the war against the Trojans. Because of the mishaps and adventures they have on the way, it takes Odysseus and his men a very long time to get home. Every place they visit seems to involve them in an adventure and Circe's island is no exception.

A few days after they land on the island, Odysseus sends off a search party to explore it. They find a fine house in a clearing right in the middle of the island. Wolves and lions are prowling round the house, but rather than attack the men, the animals rise up on their hind legs seeking attention and affection. The men can hear beautiful singing coming from inside the house: it is Circe singing, as she weaves dazzling fabric on her loom.

The men call to Circe, who invites them in for a meal. All of them go inside, except Eurylochus, leader of the group, who is suspicious. Circe gives them a fine meal, but drugs them, so that they forget Ithaca, and then touches them with her wand, turning them all into pigs.

When none of the men reappear, Eurylochus rushes back to tell Odysseus what has happened. Odysseus arms himself and sets off, determined to see what he can do for his men. On the way he meets a young man who turns out to be the god Hermes in disguise. Hermes gives Odysseus a magic herb which will protect him from Circe's magic and tells him to threaten her with his sword once the magic has failed.

Odysseus does this and wins Circe round. She agrees to turn all the pigs back into men and the whole company stay in her house, feasting and drinking for a year.

Miss Patterson was a tyrant who finally let a student drive her bats.

Miss Agnes Patterson's fifth-grade class sat rigid under the Gorgon eye of their teacher, waiting to be programmed into the next item on their tightly organised schedule. Motionlesss, backs straight, hands neatly folded on their desks, faces careful masks of respectful submission, they seemed unaware that it was the last day before Easter vacation, with school almost out and spring waiting for them beyond the open windows. The trees now lightly smudged with pink, the call of carefree birds, the rich warm smell of moist earth and new growing things seemed to hold no charm for them. Not one so much as glanced outside. Apart from discipline, there was something on the windowsill that they could not bear to look at: an empty hamster cage.

The cage awaited no new occupant. It was simply there, to remind them of their failure in their nature study project — a frippery of modern education that Miss Patterson had never quite approved of. The committee appointed to care for the little beast had forgotten to take it home with them over the Christmas vacation, and their teacher, seeing in this oversight a heaven-sent

opportunity for a stern lesson on Responsibility, had left the animal to the fate its thoughtless guardians had abandoned it to. When they came back after their holiday, they found it dead, lying on its back, eyes closed, mouth open, stiff and cold. Miss Patterson's vivid description of the torments the hamster must have suffered as it starved and thirsted to death had left most of the children in hysterical tears. One thing was sure: none of them would turn his or her eyes in the direction of that reproaching cage, no matter what marvellous events might transpire beyond the window. They sat, subdued, fully under control. When their teacher cracked the whip, they would jump.

All except Corinna.

Defiant little witch Corinna! She sat in the corner like a cat wandered in on a whim, watching what went on with a cat's inscrutable smouldering stare, or turning her attention inward to mysterious thoughts of her own. She had a reputation as a troublemaker. She had been transferred from room to room all year as teacher after teacher refused to cope with her. Her parents had been called, but they refused to discuss the problem like good parents. They said that their daughter went to school because the law required it, and let the law make her behave, if it could. It was no concern of theirs.

She had been in Miss Patterson's class for little more than a week, and though she had as yet done nothing overt, in her mere presence the group was beginning to disintegrate. The children were restless, uneasy, like sheep who scent the wolf. Her contempt for the activities in which they spent their days was obvious. She refused to answer questions when called on, did no homework, turned in blank papers; and with her example before them, the others were beginning, ever so slightly, to get out of hand.

Miss Patterson was not disturbed. She had been dealing with troublemakers for twenty years, and she knew how to break them. Her methods were not subtle, but they were effective, and Corinna had put her most effective weapon to her hand by turning in an arithmetic test with nothing on it but her name. Miss Patterson returned the tests and addressed her pupils in a voice like honey on a razor's edge.

"Elephants have giant brains, and so all those who had perfect papers are elephants. Stand up, elephants, so we can see you. . . . My, we have a lot of elephants, haven't we . . .? Mice have little brains and don't pay attention, and so they make mistakes, but they can squeeze by. Stand up, mice . . .! Fleas are little tiny parasites with no brains at all. They're really stupid. We don't have any fleas in *our* class, do we . . .? Oh, we *do* have one! Corinna didn't get one single answer on this test! She couldn't answer *any* of the questions! Stand up, Corinna. You must be a very tiny flea indeed!"

She smiled triumphantly, and looked to see Corinna crushed.

"If I'm a flea, you're an old bat."

It was unthinkable that such impertinence could be. Stunned, helplessly conscious of her mouth gone slack, her burning face, Miss Patterson sat paralysed. Transfixed by Corinna's eyes, fierce and yellow and soulless as a hawk's, she knew — how could she not have known before? How could she not have seen what she now saw so clearly? This was no child like other children.

"You are a bat," Corinna repeated ominously, her witch's eyes grown huge and luminous. She glided forward, reached the desk and slid around it like a snake. Behind her, suddenly aware, bonded with her, strengthening her with their united wills, the children converged on their teacher. They gathered around her desk, all of them staring . . .

Did they grow larger? Was it she who shrank? They loomed above her, glaring down with savage joy.

Agnes Patterson fluttered off her chair and scuttled away between their feet, screaming for help in a voice too shrill for human ears to hear. The children, shrieking their triumph, raced after her, chivvying her from corner to corner striking at her as she dove past them. Help came at last brought by the pandemonium in the room — Mr Morgan from across the hall.

"What's going on here!'

"It's our bat!" Corinna shouted. "Our nature study bat! It got away!"

"Yes, yes!" the children chorused. "We're trying to catch it and put it back in the cage!"

"Where's Miss Patterson? She should have told me she was stepping out so I could cover her . . . never mind." He pulled off his jacket and in one deft swoop captured the hysterically chittering creature and stuffed it into the cage. He closed its door and glanced at his watch. "It's nearly time for dismissal. You kids sit quiet. I'll be keeping an eye on you from my room."

They took their places and sat until the bell rang. They said nothing aloud, but gleeful eyes met and giggles were muffled behind their hands as they gloated over the small animal huddled panting at the back of its prison. When it was time to leave, they gathered their things and left silently, in impeccable order, attracting no attention to themselves and their unsupervised classroom. Corinna waited until the others had gone. She came then and stood in front of the cage. The captive shrank still further back, but there was no move to harm her.

"Good-bye, Miss Patterson," Corinna whispered. "Have a nice vacation."

She tiptoed out and closed the door behind her.

Written by Phyllis MacLennan
Illustrated by David Wong

107

Murder in the Garden

The assassin is dressed in scarlet and black. Lifting his knees high at every step, he creeps towards the unwary female who has stopped to clean something from her leg. Slowly his head tilts back. She senses something and stiffens, alert. Too late! The assassin's dagger strikes home, not once, but twice. The victim sinks to her knees. There is no escape.

Does the killer flee the scene of the crime? No fear! He settles down to eat the corpse.

"What?" you're shrieking. "What kind of revolting murderer are you talking about?"

An *assassin bug* — that's what (or who!). And he's busy tucking into a foolish young grasshopper who really should have been more careful.

In the mysterious world of insects, scenes like these are all part of the survival game. Out there in the average suburban garden there's as fierce and colourful a collection of creatures as you could ever hope to find in a tropical jungle or African veldt.

Day and night the life and death drama goes on. It never stops.

Some of the most skilful and ingenious hunters belong to the spider family. You know about webs spun between branches or across window corners and have no doubt heard about the catching techniques of trap-door and funnel web spiders. But did you know of the net-casting spider who weaves an elaborate net to toss over the top of her prey, rather the way animal-hunters do in those old Tarzan movies? Then there are that athletic band, the jumping spiders, who leap about monkey-fashion, bouncing from stem to leaf and pouncing on their prey with uncanny accuracy. And how about the spitting spider who lets fly with a sticky fluid that literally glues its victim to the spot, until the spider can amble over and quietly polish off its frantic immobile victim.

But most interesting of all is this Magnificient Spider (that's its name, it's not just an adjective) seen here letting down her trap-line, ready for a night's hunting.

Entomologists (people who study insects) are fascinated by the Magnificient Spider. This clever female attaches sticky globules to a short length of silk and turns it into a lethal weapon by using it like

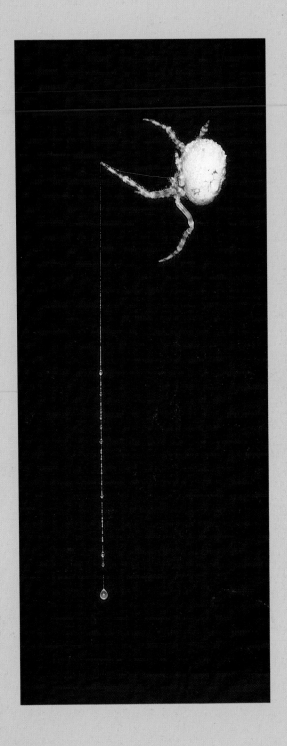

a cross between a cowboy's lasso and a fishing line. South American Indians use a weapon called a bola or bolas which has a ball tied to a cord and this is so similar, the spider is sometimes called the bolas spider.

At first the young spider will catch any suitable moth, but as she grows older she seems to get fussier. They must be only a certain kind — and they are always male. Why? Because, somehow that cunning spider is able to put out a scent identical to the one used by female moths of the same species who are looking for a mate. How does she do this? That's the mystery puzzling the entomologists.

Is the scent on the sticky globules? Or does it come from the spider? No one knows. Is it the vibration from the moth's wing-beats that tells her a possible meal is approaching? Perhaps. At any rate, she knows exactly when to start swinging that trap-line so as to catch him on the wing.

And the story ends with the eager moth encountering a pretty lady quite different from the one he thought he was about to meet, and one step off becoming moth soup!

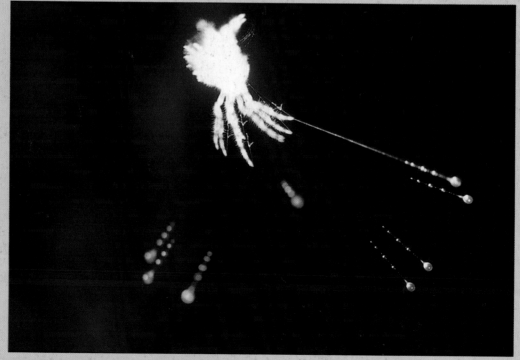

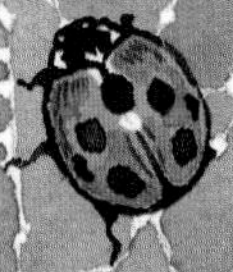

A Web of Words

Glossary

acknowledgement (*p.10*)
recognition

ambiguous (*p.5*)
doubtful, difficult to be
certain about

assassin (*p.108*)
murderer

avid (*p.38*)
interested, very keen

beseech (*p.48*)
beg or plead

chivvying (*p.107*)
pursuing or chasing

clamour (*p.56*)
noisy shouting

composure (*p.73*)
calmness

contempt (*p.105*)
lack of respect

converged (*p.106*)
joined together

crypt (*p.77*)
underground chamber

eavesdropper (*p.15*)
someone who listens to
a private conversation

fitfully (*p.64*)
not steadily

fretfully (*p.11*)
irritably

hefty (*p.13*)
sturdy, quite heavy

housewife (*p.45*)
small container for
needlework articles

impeccable (*p.107*)
faultless

impersonating (*p.84*)
pretending to be
another person

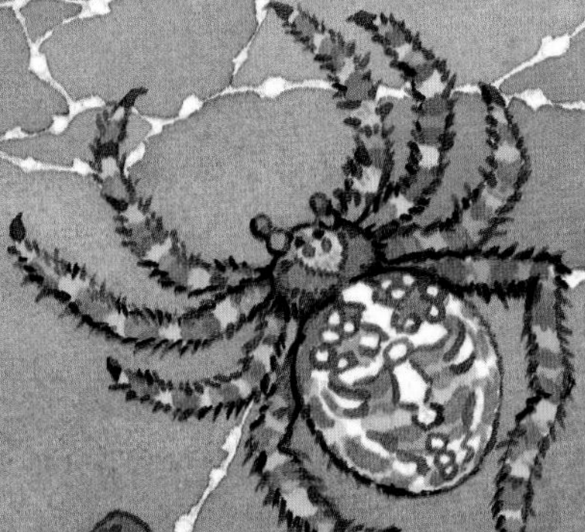

impertinence *(p.106)*
lack of respect,
rudeness

impregnable *(p.47)*
unable to be broken
into

inadvertantly *(p.96)*
without thinking

indignantly *(p.41)*
anger at something not
being right

ingenious *(p.109)*
very intelligent, clever

inscrutable *(p.105)*
mysterious

knighted *(p.39)*
given an award by
Queen or King which
allows you to become
Sir.

masquerade *(p.72)*
pretence

notorious *(p.64)*
well-known

ominously *(p.106)*
threateningly

overt *(p.105)*
noticeable

paisleys *(p.9)*
abstract curved shapes
on material

pandemonium *(p.107)*
confusion, uproar

philosophy *(p.53)*
the study of life and
what it means

prone *(p.43)*
lying flat on the ground

recommended *(p.84)*
told that a person or
thing will be helpful

relentlessly *(p.31)*
persistently, with
determination

reproaching *(p.105)*
disapproving

sashes *(p.74)*
window frames

Sedan chair *(p.56)*
portable chair for one
person which is carried
by two people using
two poles

subtle *(p.106)*
delicate, difficult to
understand

suburban *(p.108)*
outskirts of city or
large town

sullen *(p.45)*
gloomy and resentful

supernatural *(p.67)*
something unusual that
cannot be explained

surly *(p.72)*
irritable, short
tempered

toastmaster *(p.25)*
person who announces
things at a dinner

transpire *(p.105)*
happen

turmoil *(p.72)*
confusion

uncanny *(p.109)*
beyond what is
normally expected

unscathed *(p.15)*
without any injury

unwary *(p.108)*
easily fooled or
surprised

veldt *(p.108)*
open country with few
trees, found in South
Africa

vigil *(p.41)*
to keep watch

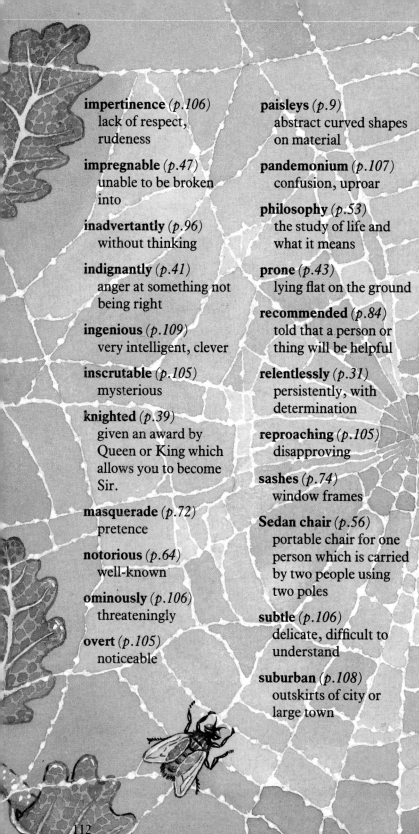